On Buddhism

On Buddhism

Keiji Nishitani

TRANSLATED BY
Seisaku Yamamoto
and
Robert E. Carter

INTRODUCTION BY
Robert E. Carter

FOREWORD BY
Jan Van Bragt

State University of New York Press

Published by
State University of New York Press, Albany

Printed in the United States of America

This work was originally published in Japanese by the Hozokan Corporation in October 1982 under the title *Bukkyou ni tsuite (On Buddhism)*. It was
included in the *Collected Works of Keiji Nishitani*, vol. 17, published in July
1990 by Shoubunsha. The present English translation of this work is from
the Hozokan edition.

The translators and the State University of New York Press thank the
Hozokan Corporation for permission to publish this work in English.

For information, address State University of New York Press,
194 Washington Avenue, Suite 305, Albany, NY 12210-2384

Production by Diane Ganeles
Marketing by Anne M. Valentine

Library of Congress Cataloging-in-Publication Data

Nishitani, Keiji, 1900–
  [Bukkyo ni tsuite. English]
  On Buddhism / Keiji Nishitani ; translated by Seisaku Yamamoto ;
translation and introduction by Robert E. Carter ; foreword by Jan Van
Bragt.
    p. cm.
  Includes bibliographical references and index.
  ISBN-13: 978-0-7914-6785-5 (hardcover : alk. paper)
  ISBN-10: 0-7914-6785-6 (hardcover : alk. paper)
  ISBN-13: 978-0-7914-6786-2 (pbk. : alk. paper)
  ISBN-10: 0-7914-6786-4 (pbk. : alk. paper)
  1. Buddhism.   I. Yamamoto, Seisaku, 1929–   II. Carter, Robert Edgar,
1937–   III. Title.

BQ4055.N5713 2006
294.3—dc22   2006003692

10 9 8 7 6 5 4 3 2 1

CONTENTS

Foreword / vii

Acknowledgments / xi

Introduction / 1

On Buddhism

Part One: On What I Think about Buddhism

Chapter 1. The "Inside" and "Outside"
of a Religious Organization / 23

Chapter 2. Opening Up the Self to the World / 47

Part Two: On the Modernization of Buddhism

Chapter 3. What Is Modernization? / 71

Chapter 4. A Departure from the "Individual" / 89

Part Three: On Conscience

Chapter 5. In Support of Human Relations / 111

Chapter 6. To Make Sure of Oneself / 131

Glossary of Japanese Terms / 157

Index / 161

FOREWORD

In these pages the reader will find a representative sample of the thinking of the older Keiji Nishitani (1900–1990), the foremost Japanese philosopher of the second half of the twentieth century.

The thought of Nishitani when he was a younger man has become rather well known in the West (especially in America)—at least in the circles of the philosophy of religion and of the ongoing Buddhist-Christian dialogue—through the following English translations of some of his major works:

> *Religion and Nothingness.* Berkeley and Los Angeles: University of California Press, 1982. (Originally published in 1961.)

> *The Self-overcoming of Nihilism.* Albany: State University of New York Press, 1990. (Originally published in 1941.)

> *Nishida Kitarō.* Berkeley and Los Angeles: University of California Press, 1991. (Originally published in 1980, but collecting material from 1936 to 1968.)

The present translation introduces a rather different Nishitani, and it may very well be that the main interest for the reader will lie precisely in these differences, which can be summarized as follows. First of all, we are offered here translations not of written and well-structured works, but of records of lectures given by Nishitani to mixed audiences. We are thus making acquaintance with Nishitani's spoken style, with all of its idiosyncrasies: frequent repetitions, a circular rather than a straight-line approach to the subject matter, and a marked tendency to digressions. If these idiosyncrasies—which are rather representative of most Japanese texts—sometimes irritate us a bit, we may find some consolation in the fact that these texts are much easier to read than the earlier translated works, which are mostly written in a fairly involved style.

Secondly, rather than directly tackling philosophical problems, the present texts present philosophical reflections on Buddhism, especially on Japanese Buddhism in its present-day situation. Knowing that Nishitani himself was, after all, a Buddhist and a practitioner of Zen, the reader may be astonished by the sharpness of the critique of Buddhism found in these pages. To cite an example: "At present Buddhism exerts practically no influence on life in society. . . . That is due to the fact that Buddhism has merged too closely into the social life, has turned into social habit, and has fallen into a state of inertia."[1]

This criticism, however, should not induce us into drawing the wrong conclusions. Nishitani certainly loved and appreciated Buddhism, especially for its power to overcome the natural self-centeredness of the human being. But this love and appreciation, far from blunting his critical spirit, rather honed it to an ever sharper edge. His criticisms are clearly intended to whip the stagnant Buddhism of his day into new life.

Thirdly, while the earlier translated works all belong to an earlier period in Nishitani's life (say, the period up to the publication of his most systematic work, *Religion and Nothingness*, 1961), the present texts belong to a later period (1975–79), when Nishitani, after retiring from Kyoto University in 1963, had already retired a second time, this time from the Buddhist Otani University (1971), but was still lecturing there. We are thus confronted with the question: can we detect in the thought of the "later Nishitani" a real evolution beyond the thought of *Religion and Nothingness*? I am inclined to answer this question in the affirmative and thereby feel bound to somehow define or characterize this difference. The scholar who first drew my attention to this evolution, Shōtō Hasa, describes the difference in the following way: "Here, alongside emptiness, one finds another major pattern of transcendence—namely, 'transcendence in the earth' . . . a transcendence finding form in what he called the Buddha Realm (*bukkokudo*), the Pure Land (*jōdo*), and also the Kingdom of God."[2] In my own words, I would tentatively say that Nishitani now pays special attention to aspects of reality to which he had not allotted full weight in his earlier system: the dark, nondiaphanous sides of human existence in its connection with the body and the earth. With regard to religion, he is now more inclined to recognize the right of these particular forms that have to do with the body and its link to the earth. And as to the human person, we may be struck by the heavy stress he now puts on the strictly individual conscience, that part of the self that is not accessible to others

("A closed chamber where others cannot look"), but is the place of a direct relationship with oneself, the place of an independence of the self that is needed for its trustworthiness and ethical responsibility. Whereas in the earlier system the whole stress lay on the individual as nonego, he now speaks of the human person as an independent "subjectivity that has at the same time a nonself nature," a "nonego-like subjectivity."

Among the elements that have evidently prompted Nishitani to this rethinking in his later years, we may mention the experience of the rejection of some basic ethical requirements by some factions of the student revolt of the 1970s and the Buddhist environment he found at Otani University, which led him to a greater openness to the symbolism or "imaging" at work in Pure Land Buddhism (and in Christianity).

Jan Van Bragt
Kyoto, Japan

Notes

1. *Nishitani keiji chosakushū* [Keiji Nishitani's Collected Works], vol. 18 (Tokyo: Sōbunsha, 1990), p. 79.

2. Shōtō Hase, "Emptiness, Thought and the Concept of the Pure Land in Nishitani," *Zen Buddhism Today*, no. 14 (1997): 66.

ACKNOWLEDGMENTS

The translators wish to thank Eoin S. Thomson of Trent University, Enomoto Yasuhiro of Kansai Gaidai University, and Deanie LaChance of Peterborough, Ontario, for their extraordinary help in looking over part or all of the manuscript, and doing so more than once. Their contributions have done much to make this book better. Thanks are due to Jan Van Bragt for his very kind foreword to this translation. The remaining deficiencies are our own.

Thanks also to Wyatt Benner and Diane Ganeles of the State University of New York Press, for their meticulous help in editing this manuscript. For his help with the index, Jerry Larock of Peterborough also deserves our thanks.

INTRODUCTION

Keiji Nishitani (1900–1990) is generally considered to have been one of the three central figures in the now famous Kyoto school, and one of Japan's most important and creative philosophers of religion. A student of Kitarō Nishida, the "founder" of the Kyoto school, Nishitani spent two years in Germany on a scholarship from the Ministry of Education. There he was able to consult with Martin Heidegger. The breadth and depth of his scholarship are abundantly evident in his *Religion and Nothingness*, a classic in modern cross-cultural philosophical inquiry, and possibly one of the more important books of the twentieth century in the philosophy of religion. As a teacher, he inspired many with his unflagging energy and the breadth and depth of his scholarship. As a man, he was generous with his time, and remarkably open-hearted and sensitive to the needs and projects of others. He delivered these six lectures to the Shin Buddhist Association of the Great Earth in Kyoto Japan.[1] The first two lectures, which attempt to lay out the problem of modernism and its effects on traditional values, were given in 1971, the second two in 1972, and the final two in 1974.

The general theme of these lectures is the depiction of the essential features of the modern age, both in Japan and in the West, and its effect on some of the essential structures of Buddhist and Japanese culture. His conviction is that modernism, which is so closely tied to the rise of science and technology, is simply unable to sustain the quality and centrality of human relationships. Nishitani emphasizes that interpersonal relationships are at the very heart of Japanese Buddhist thought and practice, and that the view of relationships arising out of Western individualism, materialism, and contractual ethics is simply insufficient as a basis for genuine authentic human relationships. His thesis is that genuine human relationships must be established on the basis of a more traditional religious or spiritual understanding. By

1

definition, then, atheistic materialism is unable to place the individual
in the wider context of the universe as a divine place and creative
source. His vision of the nature of this underlying creative source of
all things is both an attempt to retain what remains of value in the
tradition and an attempt to adapt it to the needs and challenges of the
modern and postmodern world. At the center of this interpretation is
the notion of conscience, which he takes to be the quiet bidding within
each of us that impels us to reach beyond the shrunken sense of reality
as lifeless and material, to an encounter with the fullness of reality
within our very depths. The divine as Buddha-nature is within us,
and is the aboriginal ground or source of that which is lasting in
tradition; from it arises our urge to finish what is yet unfinished: to
flesh out what is in the modern age atrophied and generally unheard
because of the louder noises of mechanization, individual success, and
material rewards. Of course, for a Buddhist, what aboriginally exists
as one's Buddha-nature is never to be thought of as a soul-like entity.
Rather, it should be thought of as a potentiality, a hidden capacity for
realizing Buddhahood. If one is able to undergo the radical transformation that eliminates the delusions of ego, soul, and ordinary understanding, then one will come to *act* as a Buddha would act. To so act
is to have realized one's Buddha-nature.

As an overview, Jan Van Bragt summarizes Nishitani's position
as follows: "It is Nishitani's conviction that Japanese traditional culture, and especially its Mahāyāna Buddhist component, carries the
necessary elements for a solution to the modern problems not only of
Japanese society, but also of western culture."[2]

Religion and the Modern World

The subject matter of these lectures, while simply expressed, is in
itself quite complex. Nishitani is concerned with finding a way for
Buddhism in particular, and for Japan more generally, to cope with its
most recent encounters with Western culture, and especially with
modern science and technology, in ways that do not neglect the great
traditions of the past. Having come under Heidegger's influence, it is
no surprise that he is concerned with the overwhelming power of
science and technology, but his approach is distinctive, because he
looks for a remedy for the difficulties posed by westernization and
modernization in the Buddhist and Japanese cultural traditions of the
past. His strategy is not to advocate a return to the past, for he is

adamant that the past is forever frozen and out of reach. Nevertheless, as human beings we carry the past with us in so many ways, and it is our task to breathe new life and significance into tradition, as it is shaped and reshaped by science, technology, and the cultures of the West. He is an advocate of change, but of a change that does not forget to carry its past into the future as an ingredient in the "mix of meaning" that quality living always demands. The authentic person is one who lives in the present with one eye on the past and the other on the future, on hope and possibility. Nishitani believes that what is required of us in the modern and postmodern world is that we simultaneously destroy and rebuild our traditional way of life in the light of the changes brought about by the secular age in which we find ourselves. Yet we must not simply join the secularists who have abandoned religion and much of tradition. They live blindly, being buffeted by the trends and fads of the moment. Moreover, they have accepted an ever present nihilism as the preferred and rational understanding of the truth of the human condition, and in doing so have lost all awareness of a sustaining metaphysical and spiritual background to our impoverished materialistic and nihilistic foreground. Nishitani's emphasis on the nihilism at the root of modernism and its worldview takes much from Nietzsche. It was Nietzsche who warned us that "God is dead," and Nishitani takes this as a warning that any of our gods, religious organizations, and lives may house an unspoken nihilism within. He is calling us to conscience, to authenticity: he demands of us that we review our beliefs in the light of the spirit of the original teachings of our traditions. In this sense, revolutionary thinking is a clarion call to return to the original teaching of the Buddha, or of Christ. Religious organizations must renew their understanding of the enlightenment teachings of their founder, lest they slide into the meaninglessness of empty ritual and recitation, or worse, into actions that are the opposite of what the founder actually demanded. As a snake renews itself by sloughing off the dead skin of its present condition, so must a tradition slough off its no-longer living traditions, and attempt to return to the original meaning and insights of its founder. Revolution is a paradoxical new look at what was, on this reading, rather than a rejection of some unchanging dogma. It is the dogma that has veered from the originary insight over the years, and now a nihilism of unengaged and uninspired followers is the result. Nishitani's understanding is that a reformer calls his people to conscience, like an Old Testament prophet, reminding them of truths only dimly remembered, if at all, and he points out their headlong rush toward the abyss of disbelief and immorality. They have lost their way, and the fastest and surest way to find it is to return to the sources of the tradition, even if not to the historical tradition itself.

Thus, it is incumbent upon religious people to step "outside" of their religious perspective, to step firmly into the modern, secular, technologically drenched age in which we do in fact find ourselves. At the same time, we must reconstruct the meaning and insight of the "inside" of our religious traditions, making them relevant to the modern age by transforming them in the light of this encounter with secularism and technology. However, this reappropriation of tradition demands that we untie the rigid knots encasing tradition.

Nishitani introduces the Japanese word *kata* to indicate that which points us toward a meaningful and appropriate way of living our lives. It is a map for action, a pattern, form, or structure for appropriate living. We must continually reconstruct our *kata* by first grasping its traditional sense and function, and then adapt it to meet and fit our new existential circumstances. Reconstruction requires, first, that we come back to origins. We need to understand once again how it is that we are to live our lives, based on religion as tradition has handed it on; and then we need to reconstruct that meaning in the light of the circumstances and conditions of our greatly changed age. And this process must continue without end. We are always reappropriating our past in the light of the present, with the hope of a more meaningful future. Nishitani refers to this as a "forward and backward movement," from tradition to technology in our age, and then from technology back to tradition in our attempt to enliven our technologically deadened world, and to loosen the rigidities of tradition at the same time. It is the establishing together of a conservative and a liberal approach to the past, and to the present and future: we must understand and preserve the past, but only in order to transform it and to rebuild from its ashes a new blend of tradition and modernism. And we must preserve the technological and scientific gains of modernism, while critiquing this secularism by means of a renewed understanding of the power and significance of tradition. It is a simultaneous conserving of tradition and a constant search for new possibilities with which to transform that very tradition.

One of the most apt and insightful images in these essays is that of the kite. It concretizes what has just been said about the importance of tradition in moving forward into a new future, and encountering new circumstances, and yet remaining true to the past. Japan, as a nation, has been buffeted by the strong winds of change; it has moved from feudalism to an age of science and technology in little more than a single generation. According to Nishitani, Japan has undergone such radical change that almost nothing has remained unchanged. Yet Japan, at least thus far, has been able to adopt and adapt to new influences, while remaining distinctively Japanese. Like a kite, Japan has been able to steer a stable course, because of the "tail" of tradition that has served to stabilize her flight into the winds of change, while being rooted or anchored by the "string" of its deep culture. A kite without the weight of tradition and rootedness simply dances wildly, becoming tangled in tree branches, or is dashed to the ground, or breaks away altogether and loses its way and its distinctive past. What here made Japan a country able to adapt to its own high-level modernization are its deep-rooted traditions. The result has been a more balanced and stable form of progress. As Nishitani explains, "[W]hen a strong wind blows, the power of tradition must be put to work. But . . . we cannot fly a kite if its tail is too heavy. It is of the utmost importance to strike a balance between these two inclinations; toward modernization and change, and toward tradition" (p. 36).

Buddhism, on the other hand, is like a kite caught in a tree, away from the winds of change. Isolated from secularization and modernization, technology and science, religion generally has been sealed away from change, leaving a huge gap between secular society and religion. The "inside" of religion has had little to do with the "outside," the secular world. And the secular world has been increasingly uninterested in religion. A central theme of these lectures is finding a way to bridge the gap, and to make religion, and Buddhism in particular, relevant to the modern world.

If religion has become isolated from the modern world, the modern world has become increasingly westernized and technologized. This way of thinking, Nishitani warns, powerful as it may be, is riddled with a sense of its own meaninglessness. It leads to the abyss of nihilism. We conceal from ourselves the abyss of nihilism and meaninglessness that Nishitani thinks is the inevitable outcome of a secularized and mechanized world, for it is both a dehumanizing force and a cutting off of the metaphysical roots that chart a path out of nihilistic despair. What we need is a pathway that leads us toward a perspective of interconnectedness with each other, the world of nature, and our ultimate source. It is his hope that the East may be able to contribute a new way of thinking, arising out of its own distinctive ways of being in the world, to allow us to confront technology in a way that will humanize technology, rather than have technology dehumanize humankind. The "premodern" may help, like the tail of a kite, to give birth to a new "post-postmodernism." But to do so, we must reappropriate the "inside" meaning of religious tradition so that from it we can find our way toward a perceiving of the worth of the human

person, the intrinsic value of nature, and the sustaining power of
our source.

Shin (Pure Land) Buddhism

As with Heidegger's "fourfold," Nishitani imagines us as mor-
tals, *in*, rather than observing, our natural environment, envisioning
the sky of ideals and possibilities, while acknowledging the "other
power" that is the ultimate creative source and sustainer of life and
physical existence (see pp. 48–50, 98). What is surprising about these
lectures is that while Nishitani stands firmly in the Zen Buddhist tradition, these lectures were presented to a Shin Buddhist organization,
and he speaks fondly of that tradition. Pure Land Buddhism recog-
nizes our complete dependence on our source. We do not sustain
ourselves in existence by our own means, at least not fundamentally,
nor did we bring ourselves into existence. Nishitani writes that we "are
all allowed to live" (p. 124) by the grace of other-power. Seiki Horen
writes, "[I]f there were no compassion toward me from the other-power
[*tariki*], my past, present, and future would not exist."[3] He goes on to
say that there are innumerable powers that protect and guide us: parents, society, nation, air, earth, sun, and, most importantly, Amida
Buddha. When reciting Namu Amida Butsu (I Take Refuge in Amida
Buddha), one needs to be grateful for this divine compassion.

Shinran (1173–1262), a founder of the Shin sect, sought a direct
way to gain religious experience, one that did not require an intellectual education or complex rituals. Recitation of the Buddha's name
leads directly to such experience, and the resultant "enlightenment"
will reveal the existence of a "Pure Land," more traditionally conceived of as a "heaven" somewhere else, but which D.T. Suzuki and
Nishitani conceive of as being right-here-now, and underfoot. Suzuki
states that the "Pure Land is right here, and those who have eyes can
see it around them. And Amida is not presiding over an ethereal para-
dise, but his Pure Land is this dirty earth itself."[4] Nishitani expresses a
similar view: "[I]t is not that we conceive of it as something fantastically
far away from us. It certainly differs absolutely from this impure world.
But I hold the view that precisely this absolute difference renders it
possible for this pure world to be established here" (p. 88).

Talk of "other-power" and dependence appears to fly in the face
of the Zen Buddhist stress on "self-power" with its assumption of the
aboriginal existence of one's own Buddha-nature. Pure Land and Zen
appear to hold competing doctrines, rather than complementary per-

spectives. And yet, to take but three important instances, Nishida, D.T. Suzuki, and Nishitani all extolled the virtues of the Pure Land tradition, and each spent considerable time studying and reflecting on the importance of Pure Land thinking in their own work. Nishida's final work[5] deals heavily with Pure Land Buddhism, and Suzuki gave a series of lectures, now published as a book entitled *Shin Buddhism: Japan's Major Religious Contribution to the West.* Nishida reminds us that although Zen teaches self-power and Pure Land other-power, they both "hold the same position. The two schools are aiming at the same ultimate truth."[6] The path to that ultimate truth is self-negation (a moving beyond the everyday ego-self), humility, or no-mindedness. It is in the depths of the self that one encounters the deep self, one's own transcendent divinity, and it is there that we encounter "the contradictory identity of the samsaric world and the world of eternal life."[7]

In fact, the juxtaposition of self-power and other-power comes as no surprise. In classical Chinese Pure Land Buddhism, self-power and other-power were thought to work in tandem. One's self-power is united with the other-power of Amitabha, yielding the "grace" of personal transformation or rebirth. This "unified practice," as it is often referred to, is a bringing together of the paths of compassion (Pure Land) and wisdom (Zen Buddhism), the two cardinal requirements of Buddhist enlightenment. During the seventeenth century, Yin-yuan Lung-chi brought the unified practice of Ch'an and Zen to Japan as Obaku Zen, a Zen sect that is still active in Japan. While Zen veered away from other-power in the centuries that followed and increasingly emphasized self-power as central, many instances of combined institutional practice could be cited.

What other-power adds to Buddhism is a pathway to enlightenment that is accessible to the common person; it is less intellectually abstract and demanding, yet it reminds one of the creative source and sustaining presence of a universal power to which any religion needs to be open. Pure Land Buddhism also reminds us, in no uncertain terms, of our sinful nature, our finiteness, our ultimate helplessness, and the sanctity of humility in one's religious pursuit. Finally, cognizance of other-power, and the limits of self-power, teaches us to let Amida work through us. The phrase "Thy will be done" seems to adequately capture this openness to divine power. One who is filled with the divine presence lives life by letting the divine work through him or her. Just as one might learn to pray without ceasing, or to recite Namu Amida Butsu tens of thousands of times a day without ceasing, so the eventual goal is to act always through the grace of other-power: it is not I who act, but God/Amida who works through me.

Buddhism and Ethics

It is often remarked by scholars in the West that Buddhism lacks a social ethics. Observing that the meaning of "ethics" is itself problematic, Nishitani suggests that ethics is "concerned with individual conscience," and the analysis of conscience is one of the central features of these lectures. Unlike the West's demand for social ethics, Buddhism's concern is with charting a rich way of life, or life map for action. He argues that at the basis of Western capitalism, including its technological and scientific successes, lies Christianity, and, in particular, Reformation Protestantism. Christianity, in all of its forms, is a historical religion: the world has a beginning, Adam and Eve sinned and were expelled from the heavenly garden, Christ appeared among us to atone for our sins, and he will return at the end of the world. Both the Renaissance and the Reformation make abundantly clear that human action is historically significant, and can and does change the world. As human beings, we act in history, and are key to the destiny of the world. It is in the world of history that we continually break down fixed forms and build new ones. The reformers of the Reformation taught us to become reformers ourselves, shapers of our own destiny, and designers of our selves and our world. Ethics arises out of an awareness of our power to change things.

It was the Renaissance, however, that provided the basis for a secularized view of the world and a secularized ethics. The West's "historical conscience" arose out of Renaissance thinking. Rather than being children of God, with a specific divine purpose, human beings were now understood to be "nothing more than" human beings. What human beings achieved was now thought to be totally under their control, and history was to be shaped by human action. Human beings were also understood to be both equal and free, and nature was to be experimented on to be understood. Humankind were now free to alter their natural environment. Human beings shape their own history, and they will shape their world.

Heaven and Earth

The Renaissance and Reformation taught that we can act to change the world, to transform it, and that we can do so on our own as active agents of change in the everyday world. But all too often, religious organizations become ego-centered, self-concerned, and self-directed. They become reluctant to share in the secular world of the general

public. Religious people must step "outside" their religious organization, as the Buddhist monks on Mount Hiei stepped down from the
mountain in order to establish a fresh Buddhism in Kamakura.

Buddhism de-emphasized this world by viewing it as a world of
suffering from which to escape. It de-emphasized time by focusing on
that which is beyond time, the transhistorical or the heaven of the
Pure Land. What Buddhists must come to do in the modern world is
to grasp that the world of time is a field, a place in which something
new continually emerges: it is a world of constant creation. History is
central in Christian thinking, and this has made it easier, if not inevitable, for a developed ethics to have arisen. But both Christianity and
Buddhism have a developed concept of *conscience*, and both have
understood it to be something deep within the human psyche that
reminds us that there is something unsettled, something unfinished or
incomplete for us to deal with. It reminds us that religious ritual and
religious dogma are but "rice cakes painted on paper" (p. 56) that
provide no nourishment for our way of living in the world. What we
require is direct knowledge, a direct experience of the divine, of heaven,
and not just unsatisfying theoretical knowing. Just as we must experience whether a drink is hot or cold with our tongue, so we must
experience directly the truth of enlightenment and have our own self-
realization of Buddha-nature: we must seek direct contact with our
ultimate religious concern. The resultant knowledge is an embodied
knowledge, a knowing of mind, heart, and soul. Faith is the indubitability resulting from such direct contact. Faith is an act of commit-
ment of the entire person, body and mind.

Christianity has the advantage of having acquired a social ethics,
much of it by borrowing from Greek and Roman thought, and elsewhere in its development. Buddhism has remained self-enclosed, leaving Confucianism and Shintoism to supply the ethical dimension in
Japan. But Christianity is similar to Buddhism in allowing its God-
centeredness to often overwhelm its this-worldly historicity. It has
often waited for the Kingdom of Heaven at the end of time, and has
seen this world as a preparation for that kingdom. Nishitani, reinter-
preting the biblical claim that the Kingdom of God is close at hand,
takes it to mean that heaven is already underfoot: it is close at hand
in that it is always already the soil on which we stand. It is not far
away, either historically or physically. The superhistorical truth of
religion must come to merge with the earth underfoot, which after all,
is the place, the space, the betweenness, the *basho* of the Kingdom of
God. The Kingdom of God has always been close at hand. For the Shin
Buddhist, the Pure Land is always already right here, right now, directly

underfoot and available. Zen, too, holds that nirvāna is samsāra: samsāra is nirvāna. Heaven is right here now, and the right-here-now is actually heavenly.

Something Unchangeable

The earth cannot be transformed unless human beings learn how to treat each other well, and the basis of human relationships is basic trust and truthfulness. It is trustworthiness that makes authentic relationships possible. Nishitani borrows from Watsuji, Buber, and Nishida in his treatment of the unchanging in human relationships. It is a distinctly Japanese perspective that he offers, demonstrating in many ways that nothing is more important to the Japanese than human relationships. Human beings come into the world as individuals, and are always already in relationship. Relationality is an utterly inescapable aspect of being human. And we are in relationship not only with our minds, but also with our bodies. We are inescapably embodied, and since our bodies occupy space, we are inescapably in some *place* of being. Formulating his position in a manner reminiscent of Watsuji, Nishitani reminds us that there is a "betweenness" between us, which both distances us as individuals and serves as the "place," or *basho*, from which we come to see ourselves either in authentic relationship with the other or as alienated and distanced from the other.

The modern world is a world of alienation, and alienation stops genuine relationships. Nishitani actually draws upon Buddhist nondualism to establish his point here; he reminds the reader that the goal of genuine human relationships is the achieving of a nonduality of self and other. Such authenticity helps to make each of us who we really are. We are more than individual egos, for there is within us another source of unchangeability. It is our Buddha-nature. He describes how Buddha-nature within is something like Buber's "I and thou" relationship. For Buber, we reach out to embrace the other as an intrinsic source of value, and in the very process of going out of ourselves, one truly becomes an "I"—that is, one truly becomes oneself. This is a notion emphasized by Nishida, for to truly know another, whether a person or a tree, one must allow the other to advance into the betweenness, and in so doing one becomes the other, since one is now fully available by having abandoned the highly structured and purposive manipulating of the other as an ego-centered self.[8] We must become the thing itself, Nishida wrote, remarking that this sense of nonduality is what the Japanese people have long yearned for, and still yearn to experience. He writes, "[T]he characteristic feature of Japanese culture . . . [lies] in moving in the direction from subject to object [environment]. Ever thoroughly negating the self and becoming the thing itself; becoming the thing itself to see; becoming the thing itself to act. To empty the self and see things, for the self to be immersed in things, "no-mindedness" [in Zen Buddhism] or effortless acceptance of the grace of Amida . . . [in True Pure Land teaching]—these, I believe, are the states we Japanese strongly yearn for."[9]

Ethics has now begun to come into focus for Nishitani. Ethics is based on trust and truthfulness, and on those authentic nondual relationships in which the other is treated as a thou to the extent that one becomes that thou. In the process, one discovers the Buddha-nature in the other and, paradoxically, in oneself at the same time. Here is to be found what is unchanging in human relationships, and it is the subjectivity of nonselfhood. It is the nondual connection with all that is. It is the connection of heaven and earth, the sacred and secular, of the I and the thou of all things.

The Individual and the Universal

It is the depth within each of us that Nishitani calls to our attention. He employs the philosophy of Søren Kierkegaard and Martin Buber in order to take the audience beyond the substance and materiality of a thing known, to the irreplaceable *subjectivity* that is known to us as our own inner awareness, the awareness that "we are" or "I am." This subjectivity, for Kierkegaard, is established fully when I, as an individual, face the Absolute. I stand alone, like Martin Luther, before the Absolute Thou. As it was conscience that impelled Luther to cry "Here I stand; I can do no other," so it is conscience that reveals the interiority of materiality. In our relationships, with the Absolute and with each other, we encounter this subjectivity, and we do so, for Nishitani, by becoming a no-self. We go out to the other and lose our self in the process, and only then are we able to enter into a relationship of mutuality—an I-thou relationship. The phrase that Nishitani quotes over and over again, that "Heaven knows and the earth also knows," I know and others know, leads us to this inner depth and subjectivity, and to conscience. Indeed, even if others do not know, heaven still does, and so do I in my depths. Conscience is relentless in reminding one that something is left unfinished.

His examples of conscience in action are helpful. The central image is that of a craftsman, a house builder who knows that the profit involved, the time and money allotted, and the details of the contract

all indicate that the building has been completed. Conscience, however, insists that there is more to be done, that even if he is to work
for nothing there is more to be done if he is to do it right. In this
knowing what is needed to complete the job the way it ought to be
completed, the artisan and the house become one. The builder so iden-
tifies with the house he is building that to look at the house is to look
at him, and to look at him is to look at the house that he has produced.
It simply cannot be left as a half-finished job. His conscience spurs
him on to do the best job possible. Nishitani compares this sense of
conscience to Socrates's *daemon*. The *daemon* warns us when we are
about to do something that we ought not to do, or when we leave
something unfinished, in Nishitani's interpretation. When it is silent,
then we have done what we ought to have done. Socrates's *daemon*
did not interfere in his decision to drink the hemlock voluntarily: he
was living, and in this case dying, in accordance with the demands of
his conscience, his "inner voice." He was in accord with who he was,
and in this sense he knew himself. "Know thyself" is here interpreted
to mean that we are living as we ought, and we are acting as our
conscience (our depths) would have us act. We are authentically who
we are, true to ourselves and to our tasks and relationships.

Science and technology, and even the primacy of substance and
basic materiality in Western culture, takes us away from the subjectivity of our "inside" self-reflectiveness, away from conscience, and
replaces it with an external, objective gaze. It is the difference between seeing a cow as a living individual and as a source of protein.
Or the difference between treating other human beings as a means
to some purpose or other, usually our own, and as a *thou*, as centers
of value in themselves. Never treat another human being merely as
a means, warns Immanuel Kant, but also as an end in himself
or herself. In true Buddhist fashion, Nishitani expands this kind of
thinking to include cows and rocks and running water, for "the I-
thou relationship obtains between one thing and another, irrespective of whether it is an ox, a bird, a stone, or even a tree. When we
love a stone or a tree, we are in the I-thou relationship with it "
(p. 96). There is an obvious Heideggerian influence here, for it is
technology that can lead us to viewing the world of nature, and even
others (and possibly even ourselves), as mere material-at-hand for
our use, as mere resources. Things become "stuff," rather than sources
of wonder and delight. Science and technology have "a tendency to
dissolve the being of individual things" (p. 98) by treating them as
resources for use, as stripped of feelings and desires, of the will to
exist. Rather than nurturing and protecting nature, we exploit it, we

pollute it, we render it alien and stripped of most of the qualities that it previously had.

What we need to understand is that nature is the field in which we are rendered capable of existing. It is our place, our home, and not only is it not separate from us, it is the very place where we, as embodied subjectivity, must live and will hopefully flourish. Nature is not mere material at hand, but is a living whole, and it is in the midst of it that we encounter the Absolute itself. All things have a common origin: all things arise from that background without form, the formless or nothingness out of which all forms, including our own, continue to emerge. It is the basis of our being. It was the source of being for our parents and our grandparents and we did not derive from our parents alone. I am born of my parents, and, at the same time, I am not born of my parents but out of the mystery of creation itself. The Buddhist notion of "interdependent origination" refers to this background of the whole out of which all of the interconnected parts emerge, or from which they derive. Nothing has a single cause, but all causes are interconnected as a multiplicity arising out of a dynamic, self-creational drive to exist.

We are both born of parents, and not born of parents. We are separate from nature, and yet we are part of nature. Nature and our bodies are not mere material objects, but are both always alive and at work. We have had to struggle against the awesome power of nature, but it has not all been struggle. The Japanese love of nature, evident in Nishitani's viewpoint here, is grounded in the awareness that we come from nature and will return to nature once more. Nature is alive, shares in the same divine kinship as a self-expressive manifestation of creativity itself, and is the place, the betweenness, where heaven and earth come together. The bodhisattva Miroku symbolizes this intersection. To be "equal to Miroku" means to be looking toward the future, yet bringing that vision to the world here and now, for we are all, always already, Buddhas. Enlightenment is the direct seeing that what we seek is already at hand. The Pure Land and the impure land intersect in this place, here and now, where "light" from each shines on the other in mutual influence: "then this must be the place where 'to be equal to Miroku' obtains" (p. 107). Heaven, nirvāna, the Pure Land of *jinen* (formless true reality) is to be found in this world, in this very place.

An Uncomfortable Pause

Nishitani's discussion of "land," pure and otherwise, is tarnished by his regrettable reference to the German phrase *Blut und Boden* (blood and soil) (see p. 123). The phrase was a rallying cry for the Nazis, whose worship of the "fatherland" served as a tool to excite the worst kind of patriotism. It would have been better if Nishitani had chosen a different phrase to make his point, perhaps from his own culture, but his aim here is not to praise the Nazis, or to encourage the rabid patriotism of Hitler's Germany. He is attempting to illustrate the strong attachment that people have to the land of their home country, and this phrase jumps out at one as an extreme instance of this attachment. More importantly, his use of this discussion of the love of the land, which is to be found in the psyche of most nations (cf. the national hymn "America the Beautiful," or the folk anthem, widely listened to in both the United States and Canada, "This Land Is Your Land, This Land Is My Land"), is intended to point us beyond nationalism, and toward the transformation of any and all land into "pure land," or heaven on earth. Even countries may have something like bad karma, from which it is not easy to shake loose. Positively, we are tied to the land by blood relations, and "soil" becomes a symbol or metaphor for the various affections and allegiances we feel for our country and its people. The land is the "rock foundation" that supports us, but the land is also "the land of God" in that every country thinks of itself as God-given, if not divinely special. Nishitani wants us to extend the significance of land yet further, as pointing toward the Kingdom of God in Christianity, and Buddha's land in Buddhism, or the Pure Land in Shin Buddhism: blood and soil lead us to an awareness of heaven.

Awareness of the land, and our deep feeling for it, is the entrée to an awareness that we are not just living on our land, but that we are allowed to live in the first place. We are connected to other human beings through "the medium of the land" (p. 124). What Nishitani searches out is the relationship between the Pure Land and our ordinary impure land. The view that Nishitani comes to take is that heaven is underfoot, and that the land underfoot is, or can become, heaven. Had he chosen another phrase to point out the extreme importance of the land in our lives, his meaning would have been both clearer and less cluttered with the baggage of Germany's karmic past, which most of us seek to keep from the foreground of our consciousness.

Conscience

Awareness that there is impurity within us, that our karma continues our imperfections, results in an inner reprimand, however much of a whisper it may be. Conscience is that which reproaches us from a private place within each of us. Yet Buddhism's seeming aloofness from this world has not encouraged conscience to expand in such a way as to serve as the foundation for a full-blown ethics. It was Confucianism that provided the relational structure for social ethics in the Far East. Nonetheless, Buddhism has long had inner resources that might have led it "down from the mountain" of aloofness, and out into the world. A distinctive feature of Nishitani's *On Buddhism* is his detailed analysis of the role and meaning of "conscience" in Buddhism. Reminiscent of Heidegger, he asserts that genuine conscience is never simply focused on the ego, but is actually a fourfold relationship. I exist by standing outside of myself, from the beginning, for the mind "is a place where things make their appearance," which is perhaps a reference to Nishida's *basho* and Heidegger's "clearing." This "place" is also where relationships are established, and the relationships are of four possible kinds. The first is the relating of self to self. It is the relationship of reflexivity, of reflecting upon who one is, and which asks whether one is living honestly, truthfully, and authentically. It urges us to truly come to know who we are, in our depths, and in so doing (as with Socrates) acknowledging what it is that we still do not know.

The second relation is with other things, but like all relationships for a Buddhist, it is paramount that one first be "empty" of ego-centeredness. One becomes a place where things may reveal themselves as they are, in their suchness or thusness. Once the ego is emptied, then we become aware that we are already out there, in the world. The third relation is with other persons. Relationships are of central importance to the Japanese, and much of their social structure is designed to serve as a fine-grade oil that eases our encounters with each other. Genuine human relationships require honesty and the development of trust. But honesty and trustworthiness are themselves manifestations of a self that knows itself, including its own ignorance and its place in the world. The three relationships are intertwined, and it appears that the previous ones are necessary if the later ones are to emerge.

The fourth relation is with the Absolute. The Absolute "supports the self, others, and things as a whole." Conscience, as knowledge, is connected to the Absolute, which, we find, is closer to us than we are to ourselves. When our minds are emptied, and egoless, we find ourselves out in the world of persons and things, and we stand in a place of disclosure, a clearing in which God/Buddha is revealed. It is not evident that conscience is, in fact, a spiritual event, for not only do we stand naked before a heaven that already knows what is in our innermost secret place, but the knowledge that conscience reveals about the self is not the revealing of the ordinary self at all, nor is this knowledge ordinary knowledge. The true self is not separated from things or persons, nor is it separate from the Absolute. The truth of this can only be gained from direct, inner, subjective experience, and this experience is a spiritual event that establishes our conscious connection with the whole of things, the totality, the Absolute.

As a self, I am an individual who is inextricably connected (interconnected) with others, with my culture and country, and with the natural environment. Nishitani's position here is not unlike that of Tetsurō Watsuji, who analyzed the notion of *ningen* (human being, person) to demonstrate that the Japanese self is both individual and social, and inescapably confronts the place of betweenness between other persons, in the midst of which a relationship can be encouraged or discouraged. Our minds, as Buddha-nature, are affiliated with and permeated by all things in the world—in the very midst of nature. The isolated individual is but a philosophical abstraction, bearing little resemblance to the egoless self of Buddhist tradition, which stands in the midst of existence and is interconnected with everything. The new, deeper self is a manifestation of Buddha/God/the Absolute. We are not separated from the Absolute, awaiting reunion, for we are always already a self-manifestation of the Absolute. Enlightenment, which is a seeing into one's own true nature, is to see one's own divinity within. We are connected to the whole of things from the start. It is in this sense that Buddha/God sustains us. We do not cause ourselves to exist, but are self-manifestations of Buddha/God, sustained as individuals, yet interconnected apertures of the Absolute, open to the entire universe.

From the Neo-Confucian school of Chu Hsi, and in particular the work of Wang Yang-ming, Nishitani takes the term *ryōshin*, which he translates as "conscience." However, he also suggests that *ryōshin* means far more than conscience; he says it also refers to the "good mind." Neo-Confucianism was not unaffected by Buddhism, even though it was critical of Buddhism for its aloofness. Neo-Confucianism is a hybrid of Confucian thought as filtered through a powerful imported and adapted Chinese Buddhism. The Neo-Confucian "good mind" is a mind that reaches far beyond the limits of human psychology, and is that which permeates all things. Nishitani remarks that this "grand-scale" usage is akin to the Buddhist notion of Buddha-nature, or Buddha-mind, the divinity in all that exists. Buddha-mind is to be understood "as being in the midst of the world in which grasses grow, flowers come into bloom, birds sing, and in which there are mountains and rivers" (p. 113). It is "a *field* which is inclusive of all the things in the world. Such a perspective is inherent in Buddhism" (p. 113 italics added). The Buddha-mind is transindividual, even cosmic, in its scope. Those Buddhist sects holding to something like a doctrine of salvation through works have generally accepted such a view of the pervasiveness of the Buddha-mind. The chief example is Zen Buddhism, which again and again pulls us back from intellectual and conceptual understanding and toward a direct experience of the world in the moment: "a willow is green and a flower is crimson" (p. 113). The green willow, in its suchness, is the Buddha-mind. The crimson flower, just as a crimson flower, is the Buddha-mind. One catches a glimpse of the divine, of heaven or the Pure Land, of the Buddha-mind itself, through directly encountering the things of this world. Nirvāna is samsāra, samsāra is nirvāna: this world is the divine world, the divine world is this world. Furthermore, the Buddha-mind, as Buddha-nature, is the center, or core, or fundamental depth of each human being and each existing thing, all of which are manifestations or self-expressions of this same Buddha-mind. Everything has Buddha-mind, because everything is Buddha-mind.

Our conscious mind is but the tip of the psychological iceberg, so to speak, and beneath this surface consciousness, there lies a hidden depth which is always already connected to the cosmos. It is always already the cosmos as a whole, and our self-consciousness is but an individualized fixation on this surface brilliance. Fundamentally, we are inescapably tied to our brothers and sisters, to the willow and the crimson flower, to the rocks and the rivers in our depths. This is the ground of Buddhist ethics, Nishitani tells us, and it is on this path of realization or enlightenment that social ethics is to be established. The Japanese word for ethics is *rinri*. *Rin* means "fellowship," or "the relationship between one human being and another" (p. 114). *Ri* is concerned with the ideal human relationship, or with what a human relationship ought to be like. Nishitani speaks of a "sacred human relationship," meaning by "sacred" that form or path along which we will come to realize our own genuineness or authenticity, by acting in the proper way in our relationships with others. Once again, we are never mere individuals, but are always already in relationship with others. The link with conscience, given this religious and metaphysical perspective, is that it is our deep Buddha-mind that pricks us into striving to become what we are capable of becoming. It is conscience, in this sense, that reminds us over and over again that something has been left undone in our relationships that we ought now to accomplish. This is a central part of what it means to be authentic, and personal authenticity is inevitably ethically drenched, for we cannot realize our own authenticity without striving to help others realize their own authenticity. Ethics is not a distant issue for us, one to be considered at our leisure. Rather, it is at the center of our own self-realization, and unless it remains at the center, our own authenticity is unrealizable. As Nishitani explains, "[W]hen it is said that we achieve being a human being, it is not only the case that we ourselves become so, but we also render other persons capable of becoming truly human as well" (p. 115). To abandon others, or to be unconcerned about the well-being of others, is also to prevent ourselves from achieving our own genuine humanity: "[T]he more one takes an attitude that shows no concern for other persons, worrying only about oneself, the farther one is from becoming a genuine human being" (p. 116). Our own authenticity is inextricably tied to our ethical interaction with others. There is simply no way to bypass ethics and still achieve our own salvation, our own authenticity.

On a Grand Scale

A significant part of the meaning of "enlightenment" is to genuinely come face to face with one's own self. It is important to keep in mind that Nishitani's understanding of "self" is a Buddhist one. We truly become ourselves when we empty our minds and allow the world to advance to us. The ego cannot be our center focus if we are to advance to authenticity; rather, we must discover our selfless no-mindedness. The self of nonselfhood is another-centered, rather than self- or ego-centered. The result is a subjectivity of no-selfhood-selflessness as a nonduality of self and other. It is an embracing, pure and simple. It is a no-mindedness that accepts others just as they are. In a true relationship, each of us reveals a place deep within ourselves where the other can reside safely—that is, where there is trust and trustworthiness. In the Socratic sense, it is a coming to know oneself. Nishitani's rendering of the Buddhist sense of conscience is that of unrelenting conscientiousness. And as with Socrates, it is a consciousness of ignorance. When we peer deeply within ourselves, we must confess that we do not know what we claim to know or pretend that we know. When we scrupulously examine our knowledge, we find that the clearest knowledge is that we do not know at all. And this not knowing is an unending spur to further introspection, resulting in a sincerity that unceasingly finds itself in others and in their protection and nurture. Nishitani's "self" is a nonegoic self, and it is a self that knows itself only through extending its boundaries to include other people; it extends even to the farthest edges of the universe. It is an expanding self, a self always already in community, and a self aware of its ancestry as a manifestation of divine creation, however that is to be understood.

Nishitani's suggestion is that if we look within ourselves, we will come to realize that our very existence is an existence given to us from beyond, that our own selfhood cannot be separated from others, and that the self is simply not egolike in its fundamental structure. The self is always already out there, with others, in the universe at large. To truly know another is to come into contact with their conscience, and through such deep contact, trust arises—from conscientiousness to conscientiousness. Trust arises between conscientious persons. Such mutuality, however, first requires that I be honest with myself. A relationship based on self-interest neither reaches such depths, nor has stability, and it quickly breaks down.

The true basis of conscientiousness, relationships, and self-knowledge is the relationship of self with "something that opens up the universe, and renders the self capable of being itself" (p. 142). This disclosure of the universe, this "on a grand scale," is the awareness that I, other persons, things, and God or Buddha are all involved together. It arises at that place which is inclusive of the whole. To know one's mind, then, is to reach that place where such a grand disclosure takes place. In that place one discovers one's true mind, one's hollow mind, one's no-mind, and thus being aware of one's connection with the totality of things, one experiences one's true basis. Conscience drives us to come to know the totality, and thereby to come to know ourselves. Just as Socrates was driven by the Delphic command "Know thyself," the Buddhist (and the Christian, too) is driven to know the self in a way that allows the no-self to arise. And the no-self is the real, the genuine and authentic self. Whether one is driven to confess, to repent, to strive to reach the limits of reason, or to seek enlightenment, one is listening to the biddings coming from the "secret room" of conscience, aware that something is still left unfinished, and like a craftsman of the spirit, one presses on-ward until one finally comes to understand by being who it is that one truly is. Such self-knowledge is unavoidably ethical, unavoidably reli-gious and spiritual, and necessarily and unrelentingly conscientious. And what may be even more important, one will have come to under-stand that heaven and earth have met, in the awesome here and now that is you, and that is I.

Robert E. Carter
Professor Emeritus
Trent University

Notes

1. The Association of the Great Earth was established by the late Ryogin Soga, a professor at Otani University in Kyoto, who is credited with having established the basic methodology for the modern study of Shin (Pure Land) Buddhist doctrines.

2. Jan Van Bragt, "Nishitani on Japanese Religiosity," in *Japanese Religiosity*, by Joseph J. Spae (Tokyo: Oriens Institute for Religious Research, n.d.).

3. Seiki Horen, preface to *Shin Buddhism*, by D. T. Suzuki (London: George Allen & Unwin, 1970), p. 9.

4. D. T. Suzuki, *Shin Buddhism* (London: George Allen & Unwin, 1970), p. 17.

5. Kitarō Nishida, *Last Writings: Nothingness and the Religious Worldview*, translated with an introduction by David A. Dilworth (Honolulu: University of Hawaii Press, 1987).

6. Ibid., p. 80.

7. Ibid., p. 88.

8. Kitarō Nishida, "The Problem of Japanese Culture," in *Sources of Japanese Tradition*, ed. Ryusaku Tsunoda, Wm. Theodore De Bary, and Donald Keene (New York: Columbia University Press, 1958), 2: 350–65. Nishida exemplifies his position by observing that "a Japanese spirit which goes to the truth of things as an identity between actuality and reality, must be one which is based on this [an "identity between self and world"]. Although I say 'goes to things,' that is not to say to go to matter. And although I say 'nature,' that is not to say objective or environmental nature. To go to things means starting from the subject, going beyond the subject, and going to the bottom of the subject. What I call the identity between actuality and reality is the realization of this absolute at the bottom of our selves, instead of considering the absolute to be in an infinite exterior. However, this does not mean to see the world subjectively, but for the self to be absolutely negated, and for the self to become empty" (p. 364).

9. Ibid., p. 362. Elaborating further, Nishida writes that "The essence of the Japanese spirit must be to become one in things and in events. It is to become one at that primal point in which there is neither self nor others."

Part One

On What I Think about Buddhism

1

The "Inside" and "Outside"
of a Religious Organization

The Present Situation of Buddhism

When it comes to my thoughts about Buddhism, I may say that they are occasioned by two things. The first is, the present situation of Japanese Buddhism; the second (not unrelated to the first) is the fact that I have been engaged all my life in philosophy—which, broadly speaking, means specializing in thinking. The contents of my thinking today are the outcome of the meeting of these two, and it is from the perspective of these two that I wish to speak.

Although I doubt that I have anything new to say regarding Buddhism's present situation, I would like to articulate my views on what I feel is relevant to this topic. Rather than focusing specifically on the separate sects of Buddhism and their various problems, I would like to concentrate attention on Buddhism in a more general sense. The issue that catches my eye is the fact that a great gap of opinion opens up between the general public and those who belong to special religious organizations. This shows in a multitude of ways. This gap is not unique to Buddhism, but at present is rather common to all religions, and is evident in Western nations, too. Thus, Buddhism is no exception here. Shintoism and Christianity must also be taken into account; and while Christianity is a religion of Western origin, I believe that the West also suffers from the same issues as are evident in Japan. I now want to discuss these issues in more detail.

To begin with the present situation, I think that among the Japanese there are many who are willing to read the Bible, or Shinran's *Tannishō* (in sharp contrast, the *Kyōgyōshinshō* is very difficult to understand), or Dōgen's *Shōbōgenzō* (this is also a difficult book, whereas the *Zuimonki* is comparatively easy to read), especially when they become interested in religion or are actively in pursuit of acquiring a religion. But even the fact that they are deeply moved by reading the Bible, or that they are attracted by coming into contact with the *Tannishō*, does not necessarily lead them to become Christians or Buddhists, or adherents of the Shin sect of Buddhism. Instead, most of them do not become believers at all.

This means that the general public finds itself in a situation in which it does not dare to accept the established individual religious organizations or sects, even though there are many things to learn there, and even though they are inspired by Buddhist doctrines or the Christian faith, by Shinran, Dōgen, or Jesus, or by the way of life to which Buddhists or Christians manage to adhere in accordance with their respective religions. As is often said in the case of Japan, a religious organization is established with the family as its basis. This has been so in Japan especially since the Tokugawa era. People involve themselves with religion through activities such as Buddhist services or funerals, which are regarded more as social customs, and these religious activities are not tied to an individual's religious self-consciousness. Here it is evident that religion does not have a firm grip on the individual person. This is connected with the fact that religion does not seem prepared to meet the religious demands of individuals at a level beyond mere social custom. I completely agree with this frequently repeated verdict. I have the impression that it is in this that various problems of great importance appear in a highly concentrated form.

The Wide Gulf between the Buddhist Organization and the General Public

It is very difficult to find the clue that will solve the problems I have just mentioned. The most basic problem is that there seems to be a great discrepancy between the attitude of those who are concerned with a religious organization and who are supposed to be responsible for carrying on the religion, and that of the general public. The term "attitude" is somewhat ambiguous here. What I have in mind is a way of living—that is to say, a direction or a form (or a way) by means of which we live our life. So I should say "direction," rather than attitude. *Kata*, a Japanese word equivalent to "form," also has the meaning of direction. When we say *izukatae*, the literal meaning of which is "whereto," we denote a direction. At the same time, it has the connotation of form. So I am sure that form and direction combine to give birth to this Japanese word *kata*. The idea here is that *ikikata* suggests a way of living one's life, that is, a direction to take in one's life.

Since "form" leads us to think of something fixed, it is better to replace it with "pattern" or "structure." A life is structured, which is to say that it has a basic form, or rather *kata,* which moves incessantly in some appropriate direction. Because of this characteristic feature of life, we can say that it possesses a definite structure, even though not simply a fixed one. With an eye on this feature of living, I referred to it above as an "attitude." And with respect to attitude, there is a great difference between those who belong to a religious organization and the general public. Briefly, people in the former category cannot expel the awareness that they belong to a religious organization even when they are engaged in thinking, seeing, or doing something else. In a sense this is inevitable. But the problem lies in the fact that they see everything from within the perspective of their religious organization, that is, from the "inside."

To speak from the standpoint of those who belong to a religious organization, it must be noted that various religious ceremonies are held. And besides this, there is a basic position taken that is characteristic of each religion—for instance, positions that are peculiar to Zen Buddhism or to the Shin sect, respectively. Generally speaking, each position can be described in terms of the articles of faith or the dogmas that express the basic doctrines distinguishing one religious sect from another. I think that any religious sect must have such dogmas. Hence, there are also sūtras (or scriptures) connected with them; Christianity has the Bible, and in the case of Buddhism, there are the specific scriptures on which each sect absolutely relies. As a result, there is within each religion or sect a study of dogma based upon its scriptures. It is in this way that a religious organization is established, which has various rituals and articles of faith. We can say that this aspect constitutes the most important nucleus of a religious organization. Here ceremony must be emphasized. I think that ceremony reveals the most ultimate and basic issues of human works and deeds. It expresses the most fundamental stance that a human being takes toward God or Buddha. For Christianity, the characteristic features lie in prayer, or in various kinds of worship. In Buddhism there are many differences, varying from sect to sect. With respect to *nembutsu* (prayers to Buddha), there are various services affiliated with them. And there are many services peculiar to the Shingon sect of Buddhism. From a religious standpoint, we can say that religious ceremonies are most important, when taken in the broad sense as the most basic form or *kata* of the various actions that a human being can undertake in the face of the Buddha.

As for the articles of faith and the study of dogma, we can say that they are established on the basis of the most fundamental *kata* by virtue of which a human being can come to see and to know. That is to say, they are extremely important items without which a religious standpoint could not be established. Hence, I think it quite natural for each religious sect to take good care of them from within its own organizational standpoint. However, the case becomes quite different if we view this matter from the standpoint of the general public. It has little interest in religious organizations as such. This means that it is not interested in the various religious activities that take place within a religious organization before Buddha or God. In other words, there appears to be a great contradiction evident in the fact that the general public is most indifferent to ceremony as a form of religious service, as well as to sectarian dogma. It is true that the general public is very pleased to read the Bible or the *Kyōgyōshinshō*, and is inspired by them. But on the other hand, when it comes to religious ceremonies or religious dogmas, it seems to me that the public has no interest in them, or rather in most cases is actually repulsed by them. This creates a basic problem. Originally, religious rituals and doctrines were thought of as having been concerned with a human being's fundamental way of life. They originated in answers to various doubts that arose gradually through confrontation with the basic problems of living. The religious demand of pursuing and answering these doubts led religions to try to find various solutions to them. At present, however, the problem is that these religious ceremonies or services are rather matters unrelated to their lives, or in some cases, are actually viewed as repulsive by the general public, and particularly by those who are in quest of religious truth in the midst of doubt. The question is, then: From what source or sources does this attitude originate?

Religion is Normally Concerned with a Human's Way of Being

Needless to say, religious services and the study of dogma have come into existence against the background of their historical traditions, and have continued to support their respective religious organizations to the present day. What is required now is to bring them back to their origins once more. Here the term "origin" refers to a place where the religious demands of a human being take root and have their beginning. These religious practices were given as a way of life itself. It is very important to bring this way of life back again to the place in which it originated. To "bring back" means to render this way of life capable of being a "living form" once again. In this way, it again becomes a way by means of which, or through which, we live our lives. I think that this is a matter so obvious that we need not elaborate further.

The important thing is to reevaluate and then reappropriate the various religious services and doctrines. "To reevaluate" seems to be a simple matter, but in truth it is difficult to do. What we must do is to submit them to reconsideration, because the manner in which we have been dealing with them thus far is no longer of use. But we cannot do this so easily, since what is at stake, basically speaking, is a concern with our way of living, and hence, we cannot reevaluate them authentically without carrying this reconsideration into the very midst of our living. This amounts to saying that we must once more get a grip on their authentic meaning—that is, we must reinterpret them in a sense. We must try to interpret, for instance, what religious services really entail, or what the doctrines with which the study of dogma deals in various fashion really mean to us right now. It is to be noted here that such reinterpretation has nothing to do with so-called scientific interpretation in which we ponder in our heads this and that. What I intend to convey by the term "interpretation" is the attempt to grasp genuine meaning in the midst of really living our own lives in one way or another. The "meaning" that is inherent in religious services or in the study of dogma is that they give expression to a human way of life. To interpret means nothing less than to "get a grip" on this meaning.

This sense of interpretation has nothing to do with the scholarly one in which one tries to ponder with one's intellect what it is that this word means or that word means, even though it eventually comes to include within itself the scholarly interpretation. But it is more important to come to grips with the meaning of religious thought in and through an intimate connection with our particular way of living. What is at stake is our way of living, and we have no choice but to grasp this meaning through actually living. This requires that those who now belong to a religious organization must come back to its origins, that is to say, to those roots or origins as disclosed and encountered wherever we dig down at our very feet, so to speak.

If this is so, then we must destroy traditions one after another, in a sense. I am afraid that the term "destroy" is perhaps inappropriate here. But when it comes to our own way of life, it seems to me that we must proceed to alter the fixed form into which it has objectified itself, and that we must alter the definite structure, form, or pattern into which religious services or doctrines have become congealed. So far as the term "destruction" is concerned, I think it comparatively easy to submit something to simple destruction. Recently, some students have behaved violently with steel clubs.[1] This kind of destruction is comparatively easy to carry out. But it does not, I am convinced, bring about a real reevaluation of the traditions. What is demanded of us is rather to untie something rigidly structured in such a way as to uncongeal it, and then to probe into exactly the form or *kata* of living that is hidden behind it. We can say that what is argued for here is some sort of decomposition. If we use a word that corresponds to the word "structure," then "destruction" is appropriate to express what I have in mind.

Even though the term "destruction" denotes breaking something to pieces, what I mean is rather a procedure somewhat different from "breaking something down" in the ordinary sense. While taking part, and living in a fixed form or *kata*, we constantly move out of it, and subject it to constant reflection—that is, we examine it by reflecting upon it. What is demanded of us is to remain inside of it and at the same time to get out of it, and vice versa. These two perspectives or viewpoints of the inside and the outside are both required. In this way, we unravel something fixed little by little and hence are able to explore the meaning that it may have originally possessed as a way of life. We cannot do this without going through our own living of it. In this way, we gradually come to understand the authentic meaning of a fixed *kata*. This is exactly what is meant by "interpretation." I admit that it is helpful for modern persons that scholars engage in obtaining various scientific interpretations, so to speak. But these interpretations are nothing but attempts made at the level of "learning" in the general sense, and have nothing to do with the position characteristic of the study of dogma, that is, with a learning about activities from the vantage point of religion. As was said before, the authentic position envisaged here lies in proceeding to destroy some fixed forms and meanings one by one, and I am sure that this destruction will result in an almost continuous construction or reconstruction of something out of itself.

An Important Aspect of Religion

To reconstruct is indeed to come back to origins. The more we get a grip on an original way of life, the more it becomes revitalized in and through our own lives. Even though we do not act consciously with "construction" as our intention, our proceeding to live our own lives entices the revitalization of an authentic way of life. This amounts to saying that a new form is thereby continuously constructed and reconstructed. Thus, the process becomes a "constructive" one.

That a religious organization can come to be provided with authentic meaning indicates that it constantly derives new constructions from its origins, that is, from the origin of its traditions. In order for a religious organization to be relied upon, this renewed attempt to reconstruct out of origins is, above all, a prerequisite. This is exactly what the general public demands of it.

I think that this demand arises not so much from individual religious organizations or sects as from (to speak more generally beyond the distinction of these sects) the religious demand involved in a universal way of living inherent in human beings, no matter whether they are Occidental or Oriental.

As mentioned above, the fact that human beings feel the need to pursue meanings through reading the Bible, the *Tannishō,* or Dōgen's writings should bring to the surface their basic way of living. We are here considering religious figures such as Shinran, Dōgen, Jesus, or anyone else who concretely embodies a basic way of living. What the general public finds in the Bible, in the *Tannishō,* and so forth, is a genuine encounter with these religious persons that takes its departure from the standpoint of a human being as such. And given these religious models, the general public searches out the path of religion, that is, of religion as a way of life. Therefore, we can say in a word that the subject matter of religion consists in a way of living by means of which a human being carries on his/her life. Since this is the basic meaning of religion, various matters concerning religious organization must be evaluated and appropriated again and again against this background.

Keeping an eye on the gap between the public and religious organizations, the question to be dealt with from the standpoint of the latter is that of reappropriation in the aforementioned sense. This reappropriation—that is, "to appropriate again and again" has a double meaning. On the one hand, it means to come back to the place from which the traditions originated, and on the other, to deconstruct traditions. And I am convinced that this sort of procedure is interpretation in the true sense. To this end, what is demanded of us is, first of all, to destroy traditions one after another, and then to attempt to come back to their origins, that is to say, to resuscitate or take up in ourselves the basic living power that is at work, lurking behind it, as a result of our own living now. In other words, the power of tradition renders our present life capable of being established in the modern world; it becomes an enabling power that authentically teaches us how to live here and now.

This double activity is demanded of us simultaneously. Otherwise, we would fall into mere destruction, on the one hand, or into mere preservation of the traditions by sticking to something traditionally fixed, on the other. Thus, we are forced to cling to a conservative position or a liberal position, both in the negative sense. But a genuine way of living arises at the place where these two things are established together, that is, the adopting of a progressive standpoint, and that of a conservative one. Here the dictum holds true: "to regress and to conserve" is to be established as congruent with "to search for novel things constantly." In fact, this is everywhere evident. For the purpose of applying this truth to religion, it is necessary for us to think from the standpoint that religion is concerned with a way of life that is peculiar to human beings.

Those Who Belong to a Religious Organization Are Required to Get Out of Their Organization

What is at issue will now surface at last. But what is actually meant by the gap between the general public and a religious organization? Those who affiliate with a religious organization usually confine themselves within it, and then try to see everything from that perspective, while the general public stands entirely outside of it. What appears here is a complete separation between the inside and the outside. The issue is not that this side would be good and that side bad. It seems to me that each of them represents a position indispensable in its own way. I am sure that those who affiliate with a religious organization stand on the foundation of a religious tradition, shouldering something of deep and great importance that has been built up inside that tradition.

The general public also seeks to return to tradition, looking for something of great importance there. But at the same time, even when we confine our argument to the case of Japan, the general public lives in the midst of the modern world, standing there, and being blown about by the winds of the world. So far as a religious organization is concerned, however, since it carries tradition on its back, I think that it is a little less exposed to the winds of the world. It seems to me that those who are so affiliated are, as it were, in an airtight room, where they are unlikely to be exposed to the winds of the world. This holds true of a religious organization, which offers a way of living to its members, no matter what positions they may otherwise hold. Those who stand outside it, however, live under the pressure of new movements in history, or at least are required to adjust themselves to them constantly.

Generally speaking, a religious organization cannot, or rather should not, simply go along with the new movements, and this is also true of the Western world. In the case of Japan in particular, this defect appears most conspicuously in Buddhism. Ever since the Meiji era, Japanese society has been undergoing rapid and continuous transformation. In comparison with the Tokugawa era, present society has suffered from sweeping situational changes, and virtually nothing has remained unchanged. It is only Buddhism that has not changed. Keeping an eye on its basic aspects, we can say that it still sticks to its old-fashioned structure. Consequently, those who belong to a religious organization are now required to get out of themselves to a borderline where the gap between society and religious organization appears in Japanese history. To come to a borderline means to stand facing both sides at once. To speak more drastically, members of a religious organization are required to step outside of their religious organization. In other words, by standing on the same terrain as the general public, they must now become of one mind with the general public. However, I do not know whether the term "mind" is appropriate here. What I am thinking about is their attitude or way of life, but this transformation is not so easily achieved as one might imagine. What members are required to do is to eliminate, one by one in and through their life decisions, that which must be termed "old-fashioned." That is, they must rid themselves of the rust or dirt affixed to their traditional way of life. It is oftentimes said that even plants and animals constantly divest themselves of something old; that is, they cast off their skin. So it is urgently necessary that those who belong to a religious organization cast off the skin of tradition in one way or another. They cannot do this except through the manner in which they live their lives.

Therefore, what is most important is the attitude or way of life through which they carry out their task, the task of taking as their own, to the extent possible, the position that is the "outside," and on which the general public stands. Perhaps an objection will be raised that an endeavor of this sort is unnecessary, because they meet this task incessantly, and without conscious effort. I agree with this opinion. But to speak the truth, this kind of endeavor is much more difficult than one thinks. For they are required to make this effort not in their heads, but in their bodies, or rather in the way in which they come to feel things. It seems extremely difficult to transform one's sensitivity in this way. I do not insist that such a transformation be suddenly achieved overnight. But I do want to say that it is necessary for them to be prepared always to turn themselves and their minds in this direction. Still, in the history of religions, this phenomenon is not as exceptional as one imagines. Even in ancient times, it often happened that those who still belonged to a temple in fact had actually left it, in a sense, while still remaining within it. To confine our argument to the history of Japan, we find that the founders of the sects of Buddhism in the Kamakura period, who had submitted themselves to religious discipline on Mt. Hiei, climbed down from that mountain. In those days, Mt. Hiei was the counterpart to the present religious organizations. The fact that they climbed down occasioned the beginning of a new Kamakura Buddhism.[2] I am convinced that this act was equivalent to stepping outside of a religious organization. It was the occurrence of a renewed attempt to reappropriate Buddhism.

By contrast, laymen cannot simply go along with Buddhism, even though they are in search of something rather like it. There is something in them that prevents them from seeking contact with a greater power, or with the deep ideas of traditional Buddhism. This is a problem with which I will try to cope in the next chapter. But if this is so, then they cannot allow themselves to enter into a religious organization, for they will feel repulsed by it, despite the fact that they may also have a desire to be involved with it. To speak of this as a general phenomenon: people can become indifferent not only to a religious organization, but also to all the affairs of religion as well. What is in vogue now is a position or a way of life in which people are interested in neither Buddhism nor Christianity, nor have they interest in any religious pursuits whatsoever.

Nonclergy and Nonlaity

The general public, while being blown by the winds of the actual world, live in the real world and bear the burden of real life. But it is not yet the case that they come into contact with religion by carrying this living of their life in the world to its extreme. Far from it, for in some cases they become quite indifferent to religion. Those who belong to religious organizations, even though they still hold onto something religious, do not have the ability to lure the general public into having an interest in it. I think this is the situation in which the world finds itself at present. In order to change this, those who belong to religious organizations are required to step out into the "outside" once more. To use old-fashioned terms such as "clergy" and "laity," they must adopt the standpoint of the laity, instead of that of the clergy.

Yet, on the other hand, if what is required of them is thought to be exhausted by stepping out, then a situation arises in which they are not different than the general public. If so, then every problem disappears. But the fact is that they are required to step out into the outside, while standing on something provided by the traditions of a religious organization. These two directions—that is, the directions of pushing the position of the clergy to its extreme, and at the same time carrying out the position of the laity to its extreme—must somehow be fused into one. In this respect, I think that the position of the Shin sect of Buddhism, when characterized in terms of "nonclergy" and "nonlaity," achieves precisely this end point. The truth seems to be this: the position of the nonclergy consists in carrying out the lay perspective to its extreme, and the position of the nonlaity consists in carrying out the perspective of the clergy to its extreme, and these two positions combine to give birth to a new stance of nonclergy and nonlaity united.

The situation is the same with the general public. The nonclergy and nonlaity are here inverted into the nonlaity and nonclergy. The positions are actually turned upside down, for, from the negation of the position of the laity, there arises the pursuit of religious enlightenment, or the religious demand. Hence, the position of the nonlaity remains in place to the end. At the same time, however, the general public are not required to actually become clergymen. To sum up, those who belong to a religious organization, on the one hand, and the general public, on the other, are required to have the same frame of mind, while pushing their respective positions to their logical conclusions, even though the direction of their intent is quite opposite. In this way, we are able to set up a sort of common ground on the basis of which we are more than likely to overcome the gap between a religious organization and the general public.

When standing on the side of a religious organization, we speak of the nonclergy and nonlaity, and conversely, we speak of the nonlaity and nonclergy when standing on the side of the general public. At the basis of both, what is involved is the same, but the direction of approach varies according to the position taken. I am convinced that it is only as a result of such positioning that a perspective arises through which both sides may come into authentic contact, or at least come to grips with each other's point of view. Let me speak in an abstract manner first of all. So far as a religious organization is concerned, reinterpretation of the basic meanings of religious services and doctrines, which constitute its most important nucleus, is required by reducing them to the way of life to which they give expression. Here the term "interpret" means for us to submit the basic meaning to reinterpretation through the living of our lives, and to grasp it in a renewed fashion. To use philosophical terminology, we can speak of "existence," which is more or less equivalent to the living of one's "life." Through this renewed grasp, we are genuinely able to give new life to tradition.

Modernization and Tradition

To speak more concretely, the question must be raised concerning what is involved in that issue which constitutes the gap between the two sides. This is a complicated issue. If we take into account the present situation of Buddhism, we cannot shut our eyes to the fact that there is some incompatibility here, and that a discrepancy exists between these two sides with regard to the question of how to grasp the form of life, that is, its pattern or structure. I said above that they differ from each other in their basic form of living. Thus, it is evident that they must do their best to fill the gap on various points. But to speak more fundamentally, since the most important thing is to fill or eliminate altogether the gap that occurs in one's form of living, it is extremely important to consider this problem by pushing the nonclergy and nonlaity mode to its logical conclusion.

Let us now turn our attention to the more concrete problems that seem to have arisen here. First of all, why does such a gap or discrepancy arise concerning one's way of living, and its direction and form? Fundamentally, I think that this is an issue that involves not so much the present situation as one's way of living itself. This issue seems to center around how to make doctrine relevant to a person's way of living in the present world—doctrine in the sense of its constituting a form of living—that has existed from the long past of traditional Buddhism right up to the present day.

In the case of Japan, this is an issue that has been continually subjected to discussion in various circles, including that of religion, under the guise of the consideration of the relationship between the modernization of Japan and her long-standing traditions. But in dealing with this, it should be observed that there is a great difference between Buddhism and other areas of inquiry. In the case of Buddhism, modernization has not yet made a clear-cut appearance. In contrast with this, in areas such as politics, economics, education, the arts, and so forth, attempts to modernize were made, and in the midst of these attempts, traditions came to be revitalized in one way or another. It is in these areas that a stepping forward to the previously discussed double direction has been achieved, however imperfectly.

The history of Japan since the Meiji era has been constituted by such a double movement in which modernization and the continuing reflection upon, or the going back upon, Japan's tradition have been constantly interwoven. On the one hand, an extremely radical and entirely new direction makes its appearance. In most cases, this direction comes to the fore in close connection with the various attempts to adopt Western culture. In addition, in the modern world, this direction proceeds by being tied to the standpoint of technology. This is not only a problem for the West, but also one with which the Eastern world as a whole must cope as well. This is the direction that Japan has taken in its straightforward path toward the future. When Japan appeared to have gone too far in the direction of bringing about this extremely hasty and new reformation, there then appeared attempts to return to the traditions of Japan and of the Eastern world. These "forward-and-backward" movements have been repeated again and again.

I think that the fact that these attempts have occurred, though in an imperfect fashion, has contributed to the great power inherent in this country. Promoting either one of these directions alone is to no avail. It is because of the fact that the weight of tradition has very definitely continued to operate somewhere within Japanese society that Japan has succeeded in enjoying a more balanced form of progress. It is useless to fly in the wind without a definite direction, as though a kite's string were cut. In such a case, the kite would be lost. Japan, however, has a string attached to her. By giving the string a pull whenever difficulties arise, she has remained well balanced and has avoided being lost altogether. The kite example reminds me that the kite itself is attached both to a string and to a tail. Without a tail, it could not fly. To return to tradition is something like attaching a tail to a kite. But since a kite is destined to fly farther and farther, it is indispensable that the wind continues to blow. But it is no good if the kite is hindered from moving by being caught in a tree.

In comparison with other countries in Asia, this cultural feature is very clearly delineated in Japan. The potentiality of Japan lay in the fact that she could adopt Western culture at a high level, by virtue of the effectiveness of the power of her own tradition, which was itself at a very high level. I hold the view that the reason why the approach that Japan takes toward Western culture is quite different from other Eastern countries such as China, India, and so forth, lies precisely in this.

That tradition was actively alive in Japan provided her with the capacity to modernize. There was no precedent in the history of the world for the rapid pace and early date of modernization that she achieved. This suggests that she has undertaken something quite risky. But there was present at all times a balance between actions and re-actions. Despite the fact that both sides of this tension have a tendency to become radicalized, she was able to walk along the path of progress by striking a balance between them, even though in a sort of zigzag pattern. It is regrettable that this could not be said of Buddhism. Like a kite caught in a tree, we must try to fly it once again from the beginning. It is quite important for us to ponder how to raise it higher and higher, once we have been able to make it fly again. On the one hand, when a strong wind blows, the power of tradition must be put to work. But on the other, we cannot fly a kite if its tail is too heavy. It is of the utmost importance to strike a balance between these two inclinations; toward modernization and change, and toward tradition.

The Modernization of the Buddhist Organization

Now, this imbalance appears in Buddhism under the guise of a delay in the modernization of its religious organization. What is the crucial issue that comes to the fore here? I think it necessary to ob-serve that the present world cannot be dealt with exclusively in terms of modernization. This means that what we are now urgently required to come to terms with, and regardless of whether we live in Japan or in some other country in the world, is the need to go beyond the various problems brought about by modernization and to deal with them in such a way that modernization will eventually be transcended.

In the case of Buddhism, we have to deal with these problems in two stages. First of all, we must come to grips with modernization. And then, in connection with this, we must further take into consid-eration problems that will be posed in and through the transition from the present to the future, after the issues arising out of modernization itself are resolved.

To begin with, it is necessary to ponder what situations arose in connection with modernization. This is so because the way of life that was produced by means of modernization turns out to be a way of life in and through which we, as well as the general public, manage to live at present. At the same time, we must consider various grave issues that make their appearance in the process of modernization, but in a new fashion. In the case of Japan, modernization has come into existence under the influence of Western culture, and yet, at the same time, the path that goes beyond modernization oversteps the framework of Western culture.

To speak in brief, we can say that modernization coincides with the period in which the Western world held sway over the civilizations and cultures of the entire world. No one denies the fact that the Western world possessed power enough to exercise such control. This power enabled Westerners to bring the period of modernization into existence. By virtue of the fact that the Western world possessed such power, the civilization or culture established by it was able to hold sway over most of the world. The present problem has to do with the fact that the world that exists outside of the framework of the West has been opened up as one world, through the medium of the power inherent in Western civilization itself. This means that more problems, which are universal in nature, will arise over and above the basic difference between the Western and the Eastern worlds. That is to say, such problems as exist worldwide have come to the fore as a result of modernization. In an attempt to solve them, we must look within the framework of the Western world itself. But their basis is not necessarily to be found solely within the Western world, which has now been put in a very difficult position. The contention here is that the present points of difficulty will remain unresolved, until the way of thinking and living peculiar to the Western world, which has contributed so significantly to the emergence of modernization, is obliged to cast off its own skin.

Occidental people must now face two contradictory demands; the demand to open up to the new world through their capacity for modernization and the demand to deal with problems with which they had no power to deal. That is to say, they were themselves required to cast off their skin. Under these circumstances, a culture based upon religion, as well as a way of living that had prevailed as such since ancient times in the Eastern world, needed to be reconsidered again as an issue. I imagine the possibility of an entirely new way of living arising that has never before made its appearance in the Western world. It may also be said that the time is ripe for providing human beings with a new possibility, one that is not likely to be found in the Western world, but instead may arise out of the positions peculiar to the Eastern world, which are often described as "premodern." From such a vantage point, one can say that the problems of the contemporary world appear in dress that is quite new. Within Buddhism, too, at least to an extent, there has opened up a new vista that deciphers from the above positions the possibility of an entirely new meaning, or at least it is pregnant with this possibility. However, in order for Buddhism to adequately respond, it is obliged to solve two problems—namely, the problem of modernization and that of postmodernization. But with regard to the latter problem, it is only by means of living through the period called "modern" that we may be able to come to grips with it at all.

Buddhism and Ethics

Buddhism has thus imposed upon itself two problems to resolve. One can say that it lags a little behind other realms or fields of cultural concern in Japan. On the other hand, when seen from another angle, Buddhism, while lagging behind, has a future before it. But it is no good simply waiting for an answer without grasping this point clearly. Buddhism must open itself, or create itself anew out of its own form of living-through, instead of merely waiting for some solution to its problems.

Let me take up one such problem. When I am engaged in philosophical problems, I must pass through Western philosophy. As a result, my observations are elicited or inspired by such a passage. From that perspective, some problems emerge when we attempt to bring Buddhism, with its long history, face to face with the issue of modernization. Let me enumerate some of them. First of all, the objection is oftentimes raised against Buddhism that it has no ethics. This is an impression that Occidental people often have when they come into contact with Buddhism.

The problem of ethics has already been raised by scholars who have themselves been engaged in the study of Buddhism. The term "ethics" refers to what Occidental people have traditionally dealt with as ethics. What they really have in mind is itself a problem. But for the time being, we can say that it is concerned with individual conscience, if we may be allowed to identify it as such. Moral consciousness arises at the deepest level of an individual's mind. Buddhism is often said not to be clear about this. At the same time, it is also said to be devoid of a "social ethics." In my opinion, what is here brought to light through these criticisms of Buddhism is not so much concerned with general problems called "conscience" or "social ethics," as it is with those bases of the Western world that lie at the deepest level of modern civilization and culture, such as politics, economics, morality, and religion. Otherwise, we cannot cope with these criticisms concretely.

A detailed explanation is not needed here. But let me illustrate with a single example. In the field of modern economics, the history of capitalism, which was brought into sufficient relief by Adam Smith, has been tied to Christianity in its origins. In particular, the capitalist position, which has taken the initiative in opening up the modern world, has had an intimate connection with the ethics of Protestantism. Protestantism is usually identified with the Reformation, which was one of the main factors in the opening up of the modern world. With regard to Buddhism, however, it is ordinarily objected that it falls short with respect to social ethics. If we take Buddhism's side, we cannot necessarily say that it falls short of manifesting any ethics. It is certainly true to say that there is no high-level civilization or culture that does not involve some ethical teaching. Otherwise, high-level civilization or culture could not have been established. But in this case, it is no good insisting that there is certainly an ethics involved, and thus enumerating its various teachings in an abstract and theoretical manner. As was just mentioned, the most important thing is to make sure that the social ethics is still at work as a power that contributes to the opening up of the modern world, and thus serves as a driving force in contemporary life. We can say of Christianity that both the economic organization identified as capitalism, as well as liberalism, which emphasizes freedom and basic human rights in politics, were brought into existence along with the Reformation, which served as their foundation.

What I am reflecting upon here is ethics as a basic motive power. When it is argued that ethics has exercised a creative power that has resulted in the production of a new economics and a new politics in the modern world, then it must be recognized that religion—Christianity, in this case—lay at its base. The power of religion was operating as one of the driving forces in opening up the modern world under the guise of the Reformation.

Historical Consciousness and Religion

I have one further thing to say. Occidental people sometimes object to Buddhism because it makes no mention of history, or, rather, because there is no evidence of historical consciousness in its doctrines. Indeed, I think that this objection hits the mark. To elaborate briefly, the phrase "historical consciousness" refers to that position through which we see history as such—that is to say, a way of thinking by means of which the ambiguities of history are brought into clear relief.

We can also describe it as the standpoint of actually seeing history. But at the same time, by keeping our eye on another aspect, we can say that this way of seeing itself becomes historical. Here two things are to be noted. On the one hand, when we follow the developments through which human beings have lived their lives, generation after generation—that is, when we retrace the footsteps of the growth of human life—we can see them in the form of history. On the other hand, in order for one to see history as history in this way, it is unavoidable that one lives and moves in history oneself. In other words, it is necessary to grasp historically the way of living-through that one lives historically. Therefore, that the historical world comes into sight for us is connected with the fact that the way of life of an individual itself turns out to be historical, and that one comes to realize that one is living a historical life oneself. I think these two things combine to give birth to historical consciousness.

I am sure that Buddhism falls short of such historical consciousness, at least to some extent. Generally speaking, something called "historical" exists no less in China than in India and Japan. But I have the impression that in these countries there has been no trace of seeing the world as history in the true sense of the word. It is repeatedly remarked that there is a historical way of thinking even in Buddhism, and that for instance, its teaching of *shōzōmatsu* (i.e., the tripartite scheme of Buddhist theory of history: the true dharma, the semblance dharma, and the declining dharma) is an attempt to grasp its development under the guise of history. Indeed, this seems persuasive. But this way of thinking is somewhat different from a historical one, at least of the sort prevalent in the modern world

The term "historical" is used in the modern world to refer to history as brought to light from the standpoint of historical consciousness. But it can be said that the history described in terms of *shōzōmatsu* is something different from this. Rather, with respect to the Western world, mention is repeatedly made of the fact that the religions prevalent there, and Christianity in particular, are to a great extent based upon history. The creation of the world by God can be said to refer to the beginning of the history of the world, and the story of Adam's purge from the Garden of Eden on the charge of having gone against God's commandment refers to the beginning of the history of mankind. Furthermore, with respect to the end of history, there is the *eschaton* of history as the Second Advent of Christ. This is a conception of the end of history in the sense that history since Adam comes to an end, and a new history begins. Here a view quite different from that of Buddhism has appeared on the scene. The difference lies in this: in

Christianity the development of mankind is cut off by its beginning and its end, and between them, history goes on from its starting point, and eventually comes to an end.

However, when viewed from another angle, Christianity's view of history can be said to be quite similar to Buddhism's idea of *shōzōmatsu*. However, the Reformation first provided the occasion to bring this view of history into sufficient relief in the form of the "historical." Such concepts as Adam's fall through sin, the atonement of this sin through the First Advent of Christ, the Second Advent of Christ—that is, Christ's death and resurrection—and the announcement of the *eschaton* of history through the Last Judgment of history in which everything from the beginning to the end is taken into account are involved in Christianity from the start. But it is through the Reformation that these concepts were delineated in a clear-cut way. Here such issues as sin and the *eschaton* were pressed forward and came sharply to the surface of consciousness. This point was made from the perspective of Protestantism, where the consciousness of history made its appearance. If we consider the Middle Ages in the West, we are certainly not justified in saying that one can find no traces of such a consciousness of history. But, in fact, whenever this sort of consciousness appeared on the scene in Christian churches in the Middle Ages, it was always branded as heretical. In the Middle Ages, Christendom was regarded as capable of eternal continuity; it was thought to be irreplaceable and to have an eternal, unchangeable, and fixed pattern. Thus, whenever a historical way of thinking came to the fore in Christianity, as it did in primeval Christianity, there was no alternative for medieval Christianity but to brand it as heretical.

The standpoint of religion with such historical characteristics as were inherent in primeval Christianity had not been brought fully to life until Protestantism came on the scene. Yet, the standpoint of Protestantism alone was not enough to give rise to the emergence of a historical consciousness. Another factor was needed to bring about this result. To illustrate this with an example, Protestantism was accompanied by secular ethics. This means that a position different from a religious one appeared on the scene as a transformation of that religious standpoint. Similarly, with respect to history, Christianity has operated as one of the basic driving forces in gradually producing the perspective of seeing things historically. As is repeatedly remarked, this is tied up with the fact that the science of history—the attempt to pursue and study history scientifically—was established. As a result, it is clear that in an attempt to take history into account, the standpoint of the science of history was brought into definite relief.

A Historical Way of Thinking and Its Practice

I do have an additional comment to make. Historical consciousness involves the understanding that we ourselves live within history. With this in mind, we can say that it is through reform or revolution that historical consciousness is brought into clear-cut relief. That is to say, it is by living through history that we come to grasp that our human activities are themselves historical. It was said above that the science of history consists in seeing these human activities historically. But if we take the position of practice, we then realize that we are able to reform historically what was constructed historically: once the realization that history is a human product dawns on us, we can accept that to reshape it in the direction that we think to be right is well within our reach. It is in this sense that the history of the modern world has consisted of reforms or revolutions. This way of thinking is also connected with the view that the essential characteristic of the human way of living in this world consists in constantly breaking down fixed forms and in building new ones. This view is one of revolution or reform.

Therefore, it is often said that present history is in the midst of a continuation of a great social revolution. In the background there lies historical consciousness, that is, a historical comprehension of the development of the life of humankind, as well as the view that true knowledge is historical. At the same time, human beings themselves live at present in the world of history. Thus, the present also has its place in history. The past occupies a position in the context of history, but if we see it from the angle of the present as well as of the future, then knowledge of the history of the past can be said to provide a new vista of the future. And in this case, the standpoint of reformation consists in the determination to build societies that can be regarded as righteous.

These two movements—that is, a historical way of thinking and the putting of it into practice—are combined into one. The "practice" can be said to be a manifestation of historical consciousness. In Marxism, too, these two aspects are made into one. But this is true not only of Marxism. "Revolution" has a broader sense: it is an attitude and a way of life that involves constant renovation, as is inherent not only in the revolution of societies, but also in all other realms. Let us consider art and philosophy. In both, there comes to the fore the fact that people are driven continually to find new forms of expression. We can say that this is the characteristic feature of the modern world.

Such an attitude seeks to break down old-fashioned ideas and ways, and to earnestly and unceasingly search for new ones. The same can be said for all human affairs. Revolution itself is confined to social revolution. But keeping an eye on the basic human ways of living, we can see operative in almost all realms a drive to bring about one advancement after another continuously, without anything being fixed, and to come up with new ideas—not only in economics and politics but also in art, learning in general and even in science. Fundamentally speaking, this characteristic is closely tied to historical consciousness.

Social Ethics, Historical Consciousness, and the Natural Sciences

I have referred to Christianity in particular in connection with the Reformation. But in fact, it is from the Renaissance that historical consciousness genuinely arose. The standpoint of the Renaissance was that of human self-realization—that is, the realization that a human being is nothing more than a human being. To the contrary, in the Middle Ages, where the existence of God was presupposed, human beings conceived of themselves as being attached to God. Religion operated from within such a standpoint. Human beings were assumed to be constantly connected with God. Since the world of nature was regarded as created by God, and since the human world and its history—that is, the constant advancement made in history—was still thought of as having been due to Divine Providence, both the world of nature and that of mankind were thought to be fundamentally determined by God.

The Renaissance standpoint was different. When they tried to see themselves, Renaissance thinkers adopted a standpoint quite apart from God. They saw human beings with *humanitas* as their axis. As a consequence, the way of thinking about history underwent a radical transformation. It turned out that what human beings had produced was now thought to have been achieved by their own power, instead of by Divine Providence. We can further assert that even the concept of God was thought to be nothing more than a human product. Thus, the way of seeing things was actually reversed. Be that as it may, man's way of thinking, and hence the pattern or structure inherent in the human way of living, underwent a radical change.

The view that history is to be dealt with as that realm in which human life is carried on finally leads us to conclude that history is capable of being produced by human beings, that it was really so produced in the past, and that it is likely to be so produced in the future. This way of thinking is intimately connected with the awareness that human beings are capable of handling things by means of their own abilities (*jiriki*), and without the need to subject themselves to God.

Moreover, the consciousness of human freedom itself was also called into question. Insofar as freedom is a human right, everyone is said to be equal with respect to their being free. Thus arise the concepts of freedom and equality. At any rate, both concepts are tied up with the awareness of human beings as their own subjects. This direction has been pursued ever since the Renaissance.

An additional significant characteristic of the modern world is the establishment of the natural sciences. The view of the world of nature came to be that of modern science. This standpoint is quite different from the way of seeing nature that had been held from ancient times to the Middle Ages. It is experimental in essence. An experiment is something connected directly with the behavior of human beings. One acts upon nature. Instead of looking on this activity from without, one tries to discover the laws of nature by entering into nature, and by moving nature from within. Thus arises a knowledge of nature from the standpoint of experimentation. This is why such knowledge is connected with human action. This standpoint consists in the contention that genuine knowledge is obtained by entering into the inside of nature, and in moving nature from within. Therefore, in this case, the sciences are connected to facts at their very foundation.

I do not have enough time to make a detailed explanation of this, but we can say that these three issues—that is, the theme of social ethics, the development of historical consciousness (and hence, the standpoint of human subjectivity), and the standpoint of the natural sciences—are the three forces that have shaped modernity.

Provided that religion is concerned with a way of living, we must conclude that it is these three perspectives that basically held sway over the way of human living inherent in the modern world. The question is: What happens, if we bring these three perspectives face to face with the Buddhist position? I think that a very basic difficulty is here posed. We must engage in this confrontation by actually entering into it, and going through it. People ordinarily tend to think that such developments as historical consciousness, social ethics, and the natural sciences are all matters that are quite difficult to deal with. The fact is, however, that their power is at work at the very foundation of our lives. The microphone and tape recorder now operating in this room are all originally dependent on the power of the sciences. And furthermore, such issues as individual subjectivity and history, are involved in what we encounter all the time on the streets and in our lives. Besides that, they are also involved in the big issues that put in motion the world as a whole. If we push problems inherent in Buddhism to their logical consequence, then we must try to engage ourselves in such issues as have just been dealt with in terms of social ethics, historical consciousness, and the natural sciences. Thus, judging from the doctrines of Buddhism, and Buddha's teachings, we can say that all of the issues so far mentioned confront one another. I think it necessary to probe the points at issue further with as much clarity as possible by standing directly on the field of this mutual confrontation.

Notes

1. At the time when Nishitani gave this lecture in 1971, the student movement was still involved in the violent protests that had begun during the 1960s. Many leftist students waged a kind of war primarily against the existence of the security treaty that the Japanese government had concluded with the United States. The students protested, wearing helmets on their heads and having "iron clubs" or "iron sticks" in their hands.

2. In the Kamakura period (from the end of the twelfth century to 1333), great religious figures such as Shinran (1173–1262), the founder of the Nichiren sect of Buddhism, decided to climb down from Mt. Hiei (where they had devoted themselves to studying Buddhist doctrines as well as to performing various religious practices) in order to establish their own distinctive and purified religious organizations.

2

Opening Up the Self to the World

Buddha, Dharma, and *Sangha*

In the preceding chapter, I dealt with the problem of how to close the large gap that exists between Buddhist religious organizations and the general public. A variety of questions emerge. Briefly, I can say that religious organizations are likely to become ego-centered—that is, that their basic attitude assumes a posture that cannot help but open them to the accusation of being religious organizations for their own sake. I have the feeling that the various problems that result may be attributed to this basic attitude. Fundamentally speaking, however, those who belong to a religious organization tend to assume such an attitude of their own accord. I am afraid that to apply the term "ego-centeredness" is to miss the mark. Rather, what I have in mind is that those people affiliated with a religious organization are reluctant to merge with and share the same feelings as the general public. In the course of things they come to assume such an attitude, without being clearly conscious of it.

Now, some Buddhists who are aware of these problems are making every effort to avoid this pitfall. The thoroughgoing accomplishment of these efforts consists in climbing down from Mt. Hiei, so to speak, as many predecessors in the Kamakura period did, as I remarked in the previous lecture. I hold the view that this climbing down must be accompanied by a fundamental transformation of attitude that consists in seeing the outside by stepping out of a religious organization, instead of maintaining the posture of seeing it from the inside. What is demanded of those who belong to a religious organization is to achieve a transformation of attitude such as this, despite the fact that they still continue to belong to a religious organization. For this purpose, they must establish a position that is characterized in terms of the nonclergy-nonlaity position all over again. This is an outline of what I talked about in the previous lecture.

I maintain that the present situation of Buddhist religious organizations can roughly be described in such a way that they are likely to become ego-centered. But in the previous lecture, I refrained from probing into this issue more thoroughly, because I did not have enough time to do so, and moreover, I thought it unnecessary to refer to it again, because I have oftentimes talked about it on other occasions. If I push this issue to its logical consequence, however, I cannot avoid the contention that in the teachings of Buddhism there are elements that force a Buddhist religious organization to endorse the present situation. Let me explain in brief. It can be said that the basic standpoint of Buddhism consists in the interconnection of the three treasures—that is, the Buddha, the dharma, and the *sangha* (i.e., the religious community of priests). In this case, it must be that Buddha and dharma are conceived of as being connected with *sangha*, and that, conversely speaking, *sangha* is, of course, conceived of in connection with the Buddha and dharma. When *sangha* is referred to, since it is a community of human beings and human beings are always to be regarded as belonging to the secular world, we are led to the conclusion that priests live in the midst of history in their community—that is, they live in time.

The phrase "to be in time" is already pregnant with problems. Fundamentally, time has something to do with being. The theme of being and nothingness constitutes a very basic issue in Buddhism. Because time is essentially involved in being, being cannot be thought of apart from time. This is also the case even in the Western world. In the contemporary world in particular, awareness of this sort is very strong . For instance, one of Heidegger's books is available under the title *Being and Time*. In other words, we can say, roughly speaking, that being is time and vice versa. As is well known, in his book titled *Shōbōgenzō*, Dōgen also speaks of being-time where being and time are combined into one and are thought to be united.

With this in mind, the phrase "to be in time" sounds somewhat strange. To give the matter more serious consideration, the term "in" in the phrase "to be in time" is already pregnant with great problems. This is because the term "to be" is already time-oriented. Therefore, if we take time concretely, we are led to the conclusion that time has to do with history. And if we think of the *sangha*, it cannot be accounted for apart from its being historical, because it is concerned with human beings. But at the same time, since the *sangha* is a religious community, the basic force of its formation must be attributed to Buddha and dharma. On the one hand, it must be that dharma is transcendent of time. On the other hand, time has an aspect susceptible to constant transition, for it always renews itself and continually manifests transient ups and downs—that is, phases of prosperity and decline. By contrast, dharma expresses that which goes beyond time, or is transhistorical. But Buddhism tries to conceive of these three aspects as connected into one, in the form of the Buddha-dharma-*sangha*. They constitute the three pillars of Buddhism. Given the standpoint of these three doctrines united into one, we can say that the characteristic feature of the Buddhist position lies in this: that superhistory and history, eternity and time, go hand in hand. Therefore, when we take history into account, we must always conceive of it as involving within itself such moments as eternity and superhistory. Conversely, it seems to be necessary to conceive of eternity and superhistory as involving within itself time and history.

A Negative Perspective on History Inherent in Buddhism

Both in the Orient and in the Occident, this sort of issue has been discussed since ancient times. History and superhistory, time and eternity, cross over and intersect with one another. This point of intersection has been called the "now," "here," or "the point of contact." As you know, to use terminology prevalent in the West, it is often termed the "moment," (that is, *Augenblick* in German). The "now," while existing in time, cuts time in a vertical way. Moreover, with respect to being, we can say that in order that it may "be" in the genuine sense of the word, it always takes the form of "to be in the present." The past does not already "be" and the future does not yet "be." Therefore, "to be" is always affiliated with "here-now." Thus, we cannot adequately account for "being" without regard to its structure such that time and eternity, history and superhistory, cross over each other in it. This also means that apart from this structure of being, we cannot conceive of the fact that a human being exists at present.

For Buddhism, I think we must take it for granted that it has pondered this question. But I cannot expel the doubt that such aspects as history and the historical characteristics of a human being have come to be blurred in the Buddhist way of thinking. One aspect that points beyond time is brought into relief very clearly, if we judge from the fact that Buddha and dharma are taken into consideration. But the other aspect—namely, that it is historical and that being is time—is comparatively neglected. Or rather I should say, if the term "neglect" is a bit of an exaggeration, it is not sufficiently developed. This is attributable to the fact that Buddhism places emphasis on the negative inherent in the contention that time is somewhat transient and that this is a world of suffering. Buddhism seems to have failed to grasp that the world of time is a field in which something new emerges without interruption.

The world of "now" is a field where something novel arises constantly, and where beings come to emerge one after another as genuinely living things. My sense of Buddhism is that, while it has made various attempts to understand the world of time as something to be negatively transcended, there have been few attempts that assume a forward-looking and mainly positive pose that regards the world as a field in which something new constantly occurs.

This seems to be because Indian thought has had little to do with history. History arises only when each of the succeeding "nows" has its own irreplaceable significance—that is, has its own date. I think that in India the view that time is dated—that is, historical time—somehow became blurred. Of course, this can be said by comparison with the case of the Occident, where the religious standpoint of a human being has been conceived of as fundamentally tied up with historicity, as is particularly conspicuous in the case of Christianity. Here the sense of history is emphatically evident. Judging from the present situation, there are in Christianity many things that Buddhism needs to learn.

Where does Buddhism fall short? As I have mentioned many times elsewhere, when it comes to the study of Buddhism, or Buddha and dharma, the history of the *sangha*—namely, the theory of Buddhist community—does not come to the fore as inseparable from Buddha and dharma. In considering the Buddha and dharma, we must also advance our argument to include the *sangha*. I am convinced that, unless we attend to the latter, dharma cannot be sufficiently accounted for, to say the least. Even if this is so, I am afraid that there had been not enough room for studying the theory of the *sangha* in the past studies of the dogma of Buddhism. Even if there had been room for it, it seems to have been presented only in the form of the Buddhist precepts.

Therefore, I think it necessary to consider the theory of the *sangha* as a problem of Buddhism proper. Of course, the Buddhist precepts are of great importance. This is why they are counted as one of the three learnings, which consist of the precepts, enlightenment, and wisdom. But it is of more importance to see that the human way of being lies at the base of the precepts, and thus of a religious community— that is, to use the popular terminology prevalent in the Shin sect of Buddhism, the community of fellow men and women sharing the same faith. That which lies at the base of the Buddhist precepts is to be understood as the human way of being. My impression is that this attempt to deal with this in essential connection with the theories of the Buddha and dharma has been given less attention in Buddhism than it really deserves. I think that this is due to the fact that a lack of historical and social consciousness has been evident in the Buddhist way of thinking about the Buddha and dharma.

Social Ethics is Weak in Buddhism

Let me be more concrete. At the time when Buddhism had made considerable progress in China and Japan, it was not quite true to say that consideration had not been given to the issue of social ethics. Yet even so, if we confine our argument only to China, it was not until Buddhism and Confucianism had combined and supplemented each other that social ethics actually came to the fore. In the case of Japan, the issue of ethics appeared on the scene when Buddhism had been syncretized with Confucianism as well as with Shintoism. In my opinion, this syncretism made it possible to provide answers to various social problems, and to meet the demands of ethics. But this sort of syncretism seems not to have sufficed to exhaustively cope with the problem at issue.

Why not? Because, to illustrate with the case of Japan, Confucianism, Buddhism, and Shintoism had been syncretized up to the Tokugawa era in such a way that Confucianism alone was primarily responsible for satisfying the demands of social ethics, whereas Buddhism was responsible for satisfying religious demands, and Shintoism for satisfying that which was concerned with the standpoint of the state (which also constitutes a part of ethics). Be this as it may, during the Meiji era, Confucianism was left out altogether. It lost the prestige that it had exercised upon the general public under the guise of ethical instruction during the Tokugawa era. By that time, the issue of ethics had become very difficult to handle, and Buddhism was forced to try to find something to counteract this loss, but these efforts were in vain. There has remained a void to be filled since that time. In place of Buddhism, various kinds of ethical thinking have been imported from the Occident, but they do not yet seem to have settled down in Japan. Even if they were to settle down, the issue of how they might be connected with Buddhism poses difficult problems.

As for Christianity, it was provided with ethics by Greek thought. Greek philosophy had probed into ethics quite deeply. When Christianity gradually began to expand its influence and entered into the domain of what came to be called the Greco-Roman world, it overcame the existing heterogeneous religions, including much of Greek thought. But at the same time, it also tried to absorb them into itself through this process of overcoming. The Middle Ages followed this same path. I hold the view that this state of affairs enabled Christianity to provide a new outlook on its own ethical thinking by absorbing almost all of the thought patterns it had conquered into the life of its churches, and metamorphosing them into a Christian ethics.

With Buddhism that simply did not happen. I do not think that the results have been only negative. But nobody can deny the historical fact that Buddhist teaching borrowed elements of its social ethics from elsewhere. I cannot get rid of the impression that this has caused difficulties in basic Buddhist attitudes for dealing with the theories of the Buddha and the dharma. To speak the truth, I think that the great studies of the doctrines of schools such as Tiantai and Hua-yen (and before them, the studies of San-lun and of the Consciousness-Only school) should of themselves have given rise to a more clearly delineated development of social ethics. There is certainly no doubt that there were various partial attempts to do so. But the attitude which should have conceived of this problem from the basic standpoint of the Buddhist three treasures—that is, the Buddha, dharma, and *sangha* as unified—did not actually emerge. There was something in Buddhism preventing it from grasping the question of how to deal with the theory of the *sangha* as an essential concern of the study of Buddhist teachings. This is why Buddhism was not particularly enthusiastic about the issue of history. Basically speaking, the study of history is concerned with a way of understanding by means of which a human being tries to grasp the nature of his or her own existence. Buddhism falls short of such historical understanding. This is now the foremost problem for Buddhism as a religious organization.

In the latter part of my previous lecture, I tried to comprehend the reason why Buddhism had failed to cope with this problem in terms of its deviation from the modern age. Now, let me turn this argument around and look at it from the side of the West. I have already pointed out that the essential features characteristic of the modern world are threefold: a historical consciousness, the importance of the issue of social ethics, and the development of the physical sciences. Westerners hold that the Orient, and Buddhism in particular, falls short on all three counts, and to a considerable extent.

The Issue of Conscience

I still remember vividly what happened more than ten years ago. Professor H. Kraemer, a well-known theologian in Holland, came to

Japan to learn about Buddhism. A dialogue took place at Otani University between him and the late Professor Daisetsu Suzuki, in which I also participated. I still recollect that Professor Kraemer repeatedly raised one question among others about the relation of the Buddhist standpoint to the issue of conscience. I have the feeling that a significant problem lurks in this important issue of conscience, which is tied up with the standpoint of the Reformation. Generally speaking, of course, the problem of conscience did not originate in the Reformation; rather, it seems to have been dealt with in various ways from ancient times, both with regard to its moral as well as its religious significance. One thing to be noted, however, is that the issue of conscience with which Martin Luther had concerned himself during the Reformation, and with which Karl Barth had earnestly dealt in the early period of his theological activities, is something quite different from what is ordinarily thought of as conscience. It involves something that cannot be disposed of by dealing with conscience alone. I am convinced that all of the above figures first conceived of the relation of God and a human being, and then tried to deal with the issue of conscience based on this relationship by pushing this relation to its logical extreme.

Consider the case of Luther. He disciplined himself by taking part in the austerities of an Augustinian monastery. Obviously, he had probed deeply into the study of theology. And though the study of theology was divided into many schools, he attempted to walk in Augustine's footsteps. As a result of his study, he came to the conclusion that Augustinianism was true. But while knowing this in his head, he could not make it his own possession—that is to say, he failed to activate it within himself. Hence, he could not wipe away the gap that emerged between it and himself. On the one hand, as a Catholic priest, he had followed in the footsteps of the saints and submitted to various disciplines while repenting his own sins. In a monastery, a priest is required to submit to quite severe discipline and to lead an ascetic life in an attempt to follow in the footsteps of the saints. The ideal of the Middle Ages was very much along these lines. Since these disciplinary practices were based upon theological studies, Luther investigated them and understood all of them to some extent, and appeared to have no doubt as to their truth. Yet, on the other hand, he suffered from being unable to appropriate such theological studies as his own. To use terminology peculiar to Buddhism, we can say that we may know the dharma with our head, but cannot make it our own to the extent that it is realized in and through our way of living. There arises a gap that appears under the guise of conscience.

For us to be able to deal with this issue successfully, "assurance" or "certainty" is needed. Luther makes mention of *Gewissen*. In German *wissen* means "to know," and the English equivalent of *Gewissen* is conscience. It is associated with the term "science," which also means "to know." The prefix *ge* or "con" refers to knowledge as a whole that is acquired synthetically instead of individually. To account for the phrase "as a whole," the standpoint from which matters of fact are taken together, no matter to what extent each of them may be implicitly religious, must be shown. The term "con" (*cum* in Latin) is originally said to mean "to gather" or "to take together." It is equivalent to *sun* in Greek. The word "conscience" is an English translation of the Greek word *suneidesis*, whose meaning also has to do with knowledge. At any rate, the original Greek word implies that things as a whole are left unsettled and uncertain, even though each of them is still likely to be understood. Here the term "certain" is equivalent to *Gewissheit* in German. It means that there is no room for doubt, uncertainty, or anxiety.

At any rate, one pursues the study of religious dogma (i.e., theology in the case of Christianity) in various fields. As a consequence, one comes to acquire knowledge, and convinces oneself by saying that "this is it" so far as knowledge is concerned. But on the whole, one's feeling of anxiety remains unsettled. Here the phrase "on the whole" seems not to be based upon any philosophical system in which the various kinds of knowledge are gathered together. In order to construct a clearly delineated system in a philosophical manner, it is required that we have a clear-cut image of the whole. But "the whole" now under consideration is somewhat different from a philosophical system. Instead, it is concerned with uncertainty arising in a way that is more fundamental than that. We have uncertainty of this sort when a shadow of a doubt, nebulous as a whole, remains at the bottom of our minds, despite the fact that we have learned and studied this or that, and consequently, we are in a position to have a clear idea of things and have no doubt about them, at least in certain respects. This means, after all, that anxiety or uncertainty still remains concerning one's existence as a human being. This also means that to look for certainty about this anxiety is a problem that we cannot dispose of simply by doing our best to exhaustively pursue learning and the study of dogma (i.e., by the pursuit of what is called in contemporary universities the study of religions). This is because we remain unsettled and uncertain about the life we live here and now—that is to say, because there is a lack of certainty about the way we live our lives.

What is Conscience?

Now, what is the issue of conscience? Fundamentally speaking, it consists in definitely realizing and firmly standing on the awareness that uncertainty remains unsettled, for we cannot, by any means, come to our authenticity even though we do our utmost to study and perform the various things expected of us. Hence, in the final analysis conscience seems to imply basically that something uncertain is left intact in the relationship between ourselves and God, if we here speak of Christianity's God.

Now, why is "conscience" spoken of in this case? Perhaps what is at issue is the self-realization of a human being as an individual. Conscience has to do with the fact that it is only the "I" who knows, even though all others do not; that it is only the "I" who catches a glimpse of its own basis, even though it is hidden to all others; and that it is only the "I" who cannot deceive itself concerning something that cannot be glimpsed by anyone else, even though one may deceive anyone else concerning it in certain respects. At the bottom of one's heart, where a person cannot be other than himself or herself as an individual, there occurs a sort of self-realization or self-knowledge with which conscience, in the religious sense, is concerned. It is similar to conscience in the moral sense.

Buddhism speaks of *fugichi*—i.e., knowledge beyond doubt, denoting certainty, so to speak. Here the term "certainty" refers not so much to the certainty of scholarly achievement, but to faith. With respect to our relationship with God, we can speak of certainty in the sense that we can truly leave ourselves to God so completely that there is no room left for doubt. Therefore, faith of this sort has been repeatedly spoken of, even in Christianity before the Reformation. Out of this trust directed toward God have developed various fields of theology. I am sure that such words as "faith" and "trust" have been used in everyday life, particularly within churches and within the monastery in particular. However, somewhat different from this sort of faith conceived of as a matter of fact is the faith with which we have thus been concerned so far. When certainty is spoken of at a place where it comes to be established as a real fact in our own existence, this certainty is evident as faith. The phrase "beyond doubt" must be understood in this sense.

Therefore, we can say that conscience consists in our definitely recognizing that something basically unsettled is left for us to deal with. What is meant here is that special situation at which we arrive through the recognition of a place where there is no room for doubt.

And it is at this place that conscience is really dealt with. This is why Luther is said to have come to the affirmation of *sola fide* apart from, or rather by denying, the previous teachings of Christianity.

The basic standpoint of "by faith alone" seems to have consisted in something similar to what I have described thus far. In other words, no matter how excellent various available teachings may be, the point at issue cannot be completely disposed of by them alone. What is left unresolved is something with which we must be concerned by ourselves— that is, the problem of whether or not we arrive at certainty in the genuinely religious sense. We must raise the question ourselves, or subject ourselves to questioning, as to whether or not we have anxiety—that is, whether we are capable of achieving assured certainty in the true sense. This is something with which only we, but not others, can be ultimately concerned. But that about which only we concern ourselves turns out to be most basic, so far as our relationship with God is concerned. This seems to be what is spoken of in terms of trust or faith.

Consequently, I think that this matter lies at the base of the "by faith alone" standpoint. And at the rear of conscience lies the standpoint of ultimate concern for a human being. On this foundation, the way is paved for this ultimate concern to be brought to bear upon society so as to become the basis out of which social ethics arises.

Religious Knowledge is Different from Discursive Thinking

In Buddhism, the same standpoint appeared as in Luther. This is also the case with Shinran as well as with Hōnen. I am convinced that they have all directly confronted such problems from which their faith was derived. Even in Zen Buddhism, mention is made of *kyōgaibetsuden*, according to which there is something directly transmitted by the Buddha at a place beyond the various Buddhist teachings. No matter how much you may engage yourself in chanting sūtras and in studying doctrines, they are nothing but rice cakes painted on paper. However many times you look at them, you cannot satisfy your appetite.

One question raised here is whether knowledge is involved, when conscience is considered. I think that it was Wang Yang-ming who placed great emphasis on the term "conscience" in the East. He seems to have taken conscience into account by standing close to Zen Buddhism, and has made repeated use of such terms as "conscience" as well as "good knowledge" and "good ability." I think that the issue of knowledge is involved here. It is not scientific knowledge. It is rather a knowledge that is only accessible to one's self. This is exactly what

Zen Buddhism describes with the term *reidanjichi,* which means that we cannot know whether water is cool or warm unless we taste it with our tongue. However many times we may hear other people talk, we cannot know from that alone what it is like for water to be cool or warm. It is not until we have had the direct experience of drinking the water ourselves that we come to know it. In my opinion, at the rear of conscience lies this "knowledge acquired only by one's self." What is only accessible and understandable to one's self implies man's most basic self-awareness. To speak more generally, it has to do with "enlightenment." In Zen Buddhism, this word is often used. To use it in a more generalized fashion, I think it is correct to say that it consists of knowledge that can be characterized as "knowledge acquired only by one's self."

For instance, we are able to acquire various kinds of knowledge by reading books, or by listening to other persons. There are many things about which we gain knowledge by being informed by our parents or teachers. Most of our knowledge about the sciences, philosophy, or even religious doctrines is acquired in these ways. But among the kinds of knowledge acquired in these ways there is now and then something of which we become aware quite suddenly. Then we come to find out that this is exactly what our teachers or parents had taught us. The same can be said not only of these familiar things but also of philosophical and religious truths at a higher level. Concerning the latter truths, there are many cases in which we come suddenly to be really convinced of them on some occasion, even though we pretended beforehand to have understood their outline through reading books. This means that we have come to know them by means of our body instead of our head—that is, by becoming a human being as a whole. It is not until we acquire knowledge in this way that we come to appropriate it truly, that is, to embody it in our body—or rather, I should say, if the term "body" leads to some misunderstanding, in the whole of us, including body and mind. The phrase "to embody something in one's body" means that it is first of all given life in such a manner that it comes to be realized in one's way of living. When we gain knowledge in this way, something makes its appearance in one way or another in our everyday life. Thus, I think it possible for something to make its appearance of its own accord without the intervention of our conscious deliberation. I am convinced that the knowledge that is acquired through embodiment is different in form from common knowledge, which has been learned through books or by some other means and is understood with our head alone. The former kind of knowledge seems to have the character of "knowledge acquired by one's self."

Knowledge, so far as it is capable of being understood by our head alone, is available to be taught to others to whatever extent you like. But even in this case, if something living is hidden behind it, it is not likely to be teachable. We have no choice but to realize it through bodily experience. In Japan, such a way of understanding has been taken as being of great importance. For example, if you apprentice with a painter, that painter does not teach you to use a paintbrush, despite the fact that he or she is able to teach this to you, if he or she wants to do so. There were many ancient cramming schools in which pupils were obliged to clean rooms, or were given some other miscellaneous and familiar task. I think this was due to the teachers' idea that not to teach them was rather of benefit to pupils. This is because knowledge that was appropriated through the pupils' seeing with their own eyes, and understanding by means of their whole bodily experience, was evaluated as a higher kind of knowledge. Religious knowledge is, after all, knowledge that is to be found in this direction. It arises when a step forward is made from the level of knowledge of the whole person, and then we come into contact with something religious, eternal, and unchangeable, which is called God, Buddha, or dharma. I am sure that there is knowledge that appears as religious knowledge. It is called enlightenment in Buddhism.

I am convinced that knowledge of this sort, in the final analysis, is involved in faith, certainty, or conscience. To appropriate it is nothing other than self-realization. It is not accessible to us, unless we know it by ourselves. Rather, it has the characteristic of coming to operate in us as something living, and as truly appropriated.

Historical Consciousness is Intrinsic to Christianity

In my opinion, faith has to do with certainty, or indubitability, and in this indubitability is involved a sort of self-awareness. The dictum "I am convinced of it" may be more appropriate, if the term "self-awareness" is too much of an exaggeration. It seems to me that something is involved in faith that is ordinarily out of reach of scientific investigation, but we are convinced of its truth from a more basic and comprehensive standpoint beyond all the realms of science. If we are allowed to describe this state of affair in terms of "enlightenment," then somewhere at the rear of faith there is such a thing as "to be fundamentally enlightened."

This enlightenment seems to be concerned with what in Buddhism is ordinarily referred to by means of the term "testimony."

Therefore, testimony is involved in faith. Of course, practice is also involved. I am certain that faith-practice-testimony is prevalent not only in the Shin sect of Buddhism, but also in Mahāyāna Buddhism in general. If this is so, then "testimony" is, I am sure, borne to our self. The reason why I mention this is my conviction that Christianity deals with the issue of conscience and on this basis comes to grips with the issue of ethics, and Buddhism should concern itself with the same ethical theme. This standpoint is directly connected with faith-practice-testimony at a level that goes beyond Buddhist precepts or anything like them. That is to say, it is an ethical standpoint that originates in conscience in the midst of a human life. In my view, the basis for this standpoint has been present in Buddhism all along. But the point here is that it did not develop to the extent of becoming ethical. In the West, mention has repeatedly been made of the community that arises from the standpoint of personality; each of its members turns out to be oneself (which is called in Christianity a personality). The concept of the brethren sharing the same faith also appears in the Shin sect of Buddhism, and there is the possibility of its being advanced toward the standpoint of social ethics based on personality, as in the West.

Let me briefly clarify the problem under consideration. I hold the view that the standpoint of the subjective self-awareness of personality has exerted great influence in the modern world. I have dealt with this problem in connection with social ethics, which cannot be separated from issues such as the above-mentioned historicity or historical consciousness. As I said in the previous lecture, out of historical consciousness have arisen various movements that continually have improved the present situation in search of a new society in which the full potential of human life is realized. This is tied up with human freedom, through which one realizes that it is up to oneself to create a new society.

From ancient times there has predominated in human history the idea of Divine Providence. If this is all that is required in order to deal with history, we are left no other choice but to fall victim to resignation, a sort of fatalism, even though it is acknowledged that this view of history has the advantage of giving a bird's eye view of the development of the human world. The view of the human world as predetermined by Divine Providence, with other factors left out of account, will result in a sense of resignation, in the bad sense of the word, and will prevent us from comprehending the matter in a thorough manner. On the other hand, we can say that to have the notion of Divine Providence is to see the movement of the world clearly. It tries not to see the movement of the world only within the human context, and, to use terminology peculiar to Buddhism, not to see the things of the threefold world only from within this world, but to see them by stepping out of this world and looking back from a place set free from the world. That is to say, it tries to look back from a standpoint away from the world and connected with God, the Absolute, who is said to be its creator. I am sure that at the back of the concept of Divine Providence lies such a bird's-eye view, which looks back at the movement of the world from the standpoint of God.

I admit that this is certainly a grand-scale doctrine. But if it is considered in itself, it will lead us to mere resignation, and that prevents its materialization as a real doctrine. What is revealed in this doctrine is something that refuses to be connected with the freedom of a human being. For this reason, however excellent this doctrine may be, it cannot be accepted except as a doctrine handed down from the past. In order for it to be realized as a living doctrine, I think it is necessary for us to bump it against ourselves, or to bump ourselves against it. I think that this is demanded of the doctrine, however excellent it may be and however long it may have been continuously handed down from the past. Otherwise, it would likely have become antiquated. So I think that the standpoint of our freedom and that of continuously rebuilding society out of ourselves are inevitably demanded here.

This means that we are advised not to stick to the doctrine of divine providence, but instead we must try to bring it back again to a place at which our freedom is established. This is a movement of our genuinely coming back to ourselves in history (including societies) as human beings, as was also the case with conscience.

The Establishment of the Science of History

Notice should be taken of the fact that this movement is launched not on the basis of knowledge, but on the basis of action—that is, of a continuously renewing action. I think that an attempt to realize one's self through such action is involved in history. The power of human freedom is taken into account here. What is implied is that a human being's way of life is constantly forward-looking. One further question to be raised concerning history, and in connection with action, is related to knowledge. It is a question of knowing what true facts are like.

In the background to the establishment of the science of history, there have been various ways of looking at history that have been traditionally handed down even to the present day. Our interests in knowing which things are authentic and which things are doubtful and our strong desire to gain mastery over genuine facts are cases in point. And standing on the facts, the science of history tries to know reasons or laws that hold sway over them. Simply speaking, these attempts seem to be scientific. Therefore, two aspects are combined in the problem of historical consciousness: the aspect of action in which a human being makes every effort to achieve his or her genuine freedom, and the aspect of knowledge in which he or she tries to know the reasons or laws controlling the facts. Hence, we can say that the problem of human concern, which consists in coming back to oneself and the attempt to genuinely know facts in the world as facts, gives rise to historical consciousness. Here the problems of the world and that of action, in which a human being subjectively exercises his or her freedom without restraint, are joined into one. For this reason, human actions are always based on the knowledge of history. What I want to assert here is that a human being in the modern world, when attempting to grasp himself or herself, tries to see himself or herself in history, and that this standpoint sees history from within by entering into it. Here the aspect of practice, in which one comes to realize oneself, is intimately connected with the attempts to grasp and to understand the world's features, just as they are.

The catchphrase "to the facts themselves" seems to give expression to a very important attitude for modern persons. Its standpoint has something in common with the standpoint of the natural sciences, as I have just noted. The basic tendency of this standpoint lies in trying to know the essential features of facts with respect to the world of nature. This means to return to the facts themselves by casting away all the ways of thinking inherent in traditional philosophies and theologies, and to see them straightforwardly by taking off all the traditional clothes, so as to come to grips with what facts really are. And from this standpoint arises in turn a new direction through which to realize one's self in the midst of nature. It appears in the form of scientific technology. This is a means of holding sway over or overcoming nature by means of technology. This means has now become a threat to mankind in the guise of environmental pollution. But looked at from a bird's-eye view, the history of mankind constitutes a struggle with nature as one of its basic aspects.

This struggle consists in the human attempt to preserve its existence by any means against the overwhelming power of nature. Since nature exhibits destructive power, human beings take pains to preserve their lives. At present, technology has made so great an advancement that we are likely to forget this side of the struggle. But if

we consider the history of mankind from the primeval period, this
struggle has clearly constituted one of the most basic problems. Hence,
we can say that in and through scientific technology, mankind gained
a victory over nature—or, if not victory, at least a successful defense
against nature. This means that human beings secured both their existence and their freedom, so to speak. Since technology and what is
called the knowledge of nature in the final analysis have originated in
these struggles, it was not until they had made gradual and steady
progress that human beings came to establish society, and to spend
their lives in ways suitable to themselves. In this way, cultures developed step by step. And there lies the basic assumption according to
which human beings were able to preserve their existence and to elevate
themselves through gradual improvement, without being swung to
and fro by nature.

The Reformation and the Renaissance

The history of mankind has been outlined in its basic structure in
the preceding chapter, and in this history the significance of technology is basic. Technology and science (i.e., knowledge about nature)
have combined into one, and have been operating in and through the
history of mankind. In this way, technology is of great concern for
human beings. However, it has given rise to new problems in the
modern world. If all of these things are taken into account, we can say
that the standpoint of science consists in knowledge about the world
of nature, as well as in the question of how human beings can realize
their own freedom when faced by the world of nature. A human
being's action is itself nothing other than technology.

With respect to this action, there have been, briefly speaking, three
great movements in the recent world. One of them was the movement
of the Reformation initiated by Luther. The second was the Renaissance, which gave rise to historical consciousness. It was only through
this latter movement that human beings came to realize the position
of their humanity. This state of affair was tied up with historical consciousness. The third was the establishment of the modern natural
sciences. It can be said that these three great movements have contributed significantly to the formation of the modern world. What has
permeated all of them is the "knowledge acquired by one's self," that
is to say, the awareness of one's own existence. I cannot provide a
longer and more detailed explanation of this now. However, I am
convinced that this point carries great weight in the modern world. It

is the fact that human beings have increasingly become aware of themselves in the process of modernization.

Let me speak of this briefly. Even when we reflect upon Buddhism, I think that "knowledge acquired by one's self" has a certain weight. But in Buddhism, there is something that hinders it from coming out into the actual world of society or history. What is demanded of us as most important is to possess that knowledge which appears under the guise of "conscience," and which can be designated as "enlightenment," when understood in the wide sense of the word. It also has to do with the standpoint concerning which we are able to persuade ourselves with regard to our own existence that it is all right, or that we have understood it. Of great concern in the contemporary world is our effort to set forth and promote this standpoint by bringing it to its logical conclusion. And the point with respect to Buddhism is that this standpoint, despite the fact that it clearly lies at the basis of Buddhism, is hampered from surfacing. The reason for it seems to be as follows. As was said before, the two aspects—that is, the aspect of "knowledge acquired by one's self" and that of knowledge of the world—are closely connected. And this connection stands out in clear relief in historical consciousness. In Buddhism, however, some problems are left unresolved concerning this connection.

On the one hand, there is the standpoint in which human beings come to realize themselves as such, and in which they return back to themselves through freedom or action. And this standpoint was initiated in and through the Renaissance. On the other hand, there is the standpoint from which we come to know the world. I am sure that these two standpoints can be combined into one. The same thing can also be said of the standpoint of the sciences and technology, which are concerned with the world of nature. The knowledge of the world and the knowledge acquired by one's self combine to give birth to this standpoint. So far as Buddhism is concerned, some problems remain unresolved with regard to this point of connection. From the standpoint of Buddhism, whose modernization is impeded, the position of "knowledge acquired by one's self" and that of knowing the world are not interwoven. There is no doubt about this. In Buddhism, there is certainly the standpoint of "knowledge acquired by one's self," which we can describe in terms of "conscience." But it is hampered from coming to the fore under the guise of social ethics or of historical consciousness. Or rather, it does not come to be tied up with the sciences.

For this reason, I think that Buddhism, when it confronts the problem of modernization, is required to develop itself in such a manner that it accepts these various standpoints within its ken. With

regard to Christianity, it can be said that the relationship between God
and human beings was established in the modern world under the
guise of faith. I think it all right to say that even here faith is based on
the basic standpoint of "knowledge acquired by one's self," concerning whether something is cool or warm. But Christianity is burdened
with a heavy problem in that this knowledge is not likely to be connected with the knowledge of the world. I am sure that this is the
basic reason why Christianity has undergone a gradual decline in the
modern world. The connection between God and a human being is
here dealt with in separation from the problem of the knowledge of
the world. Knowledge of this sort does not here enter in the sense in
which it is dealt with in the modern world. The meaning of this verdict is that Christianity's posture is backward-looking. There is an
attempt to return to God—that is, the connection with God is here
entirely overwhelming. As a result, there is no possibility than that we
regard the fact of our living in this world as something negative.
Judging from the standpoint of Christianity, we can describe this
posture as God-centeredness. As a religious standpoint, it is naturally
warranted. However, if Christianity intends to be world Christianity,
as K. Barth pointed out, I am afraid that this concept of God-
centeredness could turn out to be a pitfall. If Christianity falls victim
to it, there is the possibility of this God-centeredness not being vital-
ized in the manner in which it was truly intended. No objection can
be raised against man's attempt to return to God, but I am afraid that
this attempt is likely to lead to an ego-centered standpoint, or, if we
confine our argument to a religious organization, then once again it
leads to an ego-centered standpoint.

There is ample room here to look at the world negatively or an-
tagonistically. This posture consists in looking at the outside from the
inside of a religious organization, as I mentioned above. It looks something like the posture from which we see the outside through the
window of a castle. In other words, if we concern ourselves only with
God-centeredness, it will turn out to be a centeredness associated with
a religious organization, or it will allure those who belong to it into
ego-centeredness, in a sense. This is why I spoke of a pitfall.

Religion is Originally Connected with the Earth

In order to avoid this predicament, what shall we do? Ego-
centeredness is a posture in which we shut ourselves up within ourselves. Here human beings assume the attitude of being confined to

themselves, with their relationship to God as their axis. In order not to fall victim in this way, it seems inevitable that a world standpoint must clearly emerge, and a standpoint in which human beings are opened up to this world. The phrase "to open up" indicates, after all, that we are required to open up to the world, or rather to go out into the place where the world (of nature as well as of history) is opened up, in order that our self-awareness may be given life in the genuine sense of the word. In this way, I am sure that the standpoint of faith can be truly realized without its turning out to be a pitfall.

In order for the gap between a religious organization and the general public to be filled in, I think it is necessary for us to look for this "opened standpoint" in which man's historical self-awareness is connected with knowledge of the world. I was informed that many in this audience participate in a circle called the Association of the Great Earth. I would like to ask you what "the earth" means here, or in what sense this word is being used. I think it very important to deal with this issue, but I am afraid that we do not have enough time to do so as fully as it deserves.

I think that the 'earth' is to be counted among the great elements— i.e., earth, water, fire, and wind—and that it is also connected with the problem of "land." These are the elements which constitute not only nature, but also the world. They are susceptible to being treated scientifically, and at the same time are referred to in various senses, since they are regarded in Buddhism as the four great agents. In the Shingon sect of Buddhism in particular, they are treated as manifestations of the Buddhas just as they are. Nevertheless, I think that our ordinary treatment of them is scientific in its way of thinking.

For instance, it is ordinarily thought that human beings return to dust upon dying. Scientifically, this means that the four great agents dissolve and return to dust, that is to say, to the great world of nature. In this sense, the earth is here taken into account. According to the scientific way of thinking, human beings turn out to be something like matter. Is this truly so? Someone expresses his dying wish to have his remains poured into the Kamo River and to let the fishes eat them. This way of thinking has something in common with the saying that human beings return to dust. I think that what is assumed here is a return to the land. This assumption arises in connection with the concept of death, understood in the sense that it is better to leave one's remains to be eaten by the fishes, since one's body will return to dust in any case. This way of thinking is affiliated with the standpoint of science. According to Buddhism, the four great agents combine for a time to give birth to a human body. It is here supposed that, once they are dissolved, they return to the source from which they came. So "earth" is intended in various ways.

This view is connected with life. Moreover, the concept of dust (or land) is also connected with the land of the country. In Buddhism, the Land of the Buddhas is spoken of, and in Christianity, heaven or the Kingdom of God is spoken of. In other words, it is a place that supports the existence of human beings. In my opinion, whenever reference is made to land, whether what is spoken of is the Land of Buddhas or of the Kingdom of God, a big problem is created. Since mention is made of the Land of Buddha's Body in Buddhism, the problem of land has been taken into account in various ways. Here mention is also made of the impure land or the Pure Land. The impure land is the mundane world in which human bodies are alive. And the Pure Land is said to be a transcendent sphere distinct from it. While living, we are very much in need of land. No matter how impure it may be, our existence cannot support itself in midair. It is thinkable that the dead to wander around, floating in midair in death. But insofar as we are living, we have no choice but to set our feet on the soil. It is repeatedly remarked in Zen Buddhism that even when regaining our footing after tumbling down, we must rely on the ground, for otherwise we could neither tumble down nor get up again. The soil is needed in this sense.

As for the Pure Land, it suggests a transcendence from the soil, as is the case with heaven or the Kingdom of God. But when it is said to be "land," it is almost impossible for us to take this land at its face value. It rather seems to indicate the place where existence is established, instead of a mere physical element. With this in view, we can account for such themes as hell and heaven.

The Corrupt and Vile World *sive* the Pure Land

One further thing to be noted here is the Buddhist remark that bodhisattvas spring forth from the ground. According to a chapter in the *Lotus Sūtra*, it is said that countless bodhisattvas gushed from the ground when Buddha preached his truth. Regarding these bodhisattvas springing from the ground, the explanation is that they had in fact come together for the purpose of listening to Buddha even before his emergence into this world. They are said to have existed before the world was established, and to have gushed from the ground, because they heard that Buddha would preach in this world.

In this case, I am sure that the term "ground" indicates the ground belonging to the threefold world referred to in Buddhism. In spite of this fact, it is here appropriate to emphasize that Bodhisattvas gushed forth from the bottom of this earth. I have the impression that this way of thinking is somewhat different from the view that heaven or the Pure Land exist somewhere far away from here. Nor is it a scientific way of thinking.

In my opinion, there are three views concerning the earth, roughly speaking. The earth is entirely different from the notion of land, when the impure land is spoken of. Rather, it indicates the place where we now live, that is, upon which we now set foot. When we live, we do so by setting our feet upon the earth. This way of thinking seems to be very forward-looking. To say the least, it is quite different from a desire to fly to some other place than this world, if that were possible.

When earth, or *Erde* in German, is spoken of in the West, it implies this, in its modernized sense. This is evident in such thinkers as Dostoevsky and Nietzsche. From the earth, about which these people talk, we get the impression that it is entirely different from the traditional view of Christianity. So far as our first impression is concerned, this is so. But what happens when we subject it to further philosophical investigation? I am convinced that even here the notion of earth is pregnant with problems and is worthy of further consideration.

In my opinion, the notion of earth as mentioned here is entirely different from the Pure Land, heaven, or the Kingdom of God understood in their traditional senses. Even though "the Kingdom of God" is here spoken of, Jesus's preaching about it has a somewhat different nuance, for he says that "the kingdom of God is close at hand." What is here said is that the "Kingdom of God" is approaching. This is quite different from what is historically said about "the arrival of the Kingdom of God." As time went on, however, the notion of "the Kingdom of God" gradually came to induce us to think that it exists above us in heaven. The notion of earth seems to be greatly different from the Kingdom of God understood in its traditional sense. By saying this, however, we cannot deny that it either does not have the meaning of the soil with which the sciences deal in a materialistic fashion, or is different from the traditional meaning of extended earth, as when earth, water, fire, and wind are spoken of. If the notion of earth is meant to refer to materialistic soil or to extended earth, we need not deliberately use such a phrase as "the great earth" in reference to it. But, on the other hand, if you insist that there are no materialistic implications here, you would simply not be correct. The term "earth" is used here to refer to the place from whence we came to be born, and whither we go to die. In other words, it is the place in which "to be born" and "to die" are located.

What is in fact being asked here? The real issue we are now confronting seems not yet to be brought into clear relief. What I really want to do is to activate Buddhist truth in such a way that "knowledge acquired by one's self," human self-awareness, and knowledge of the world are synthesized. I wish to maintain firmly that human existence is historical and thereby to resuscitate the standpoint of Buddhist truth, which consists in being superhistorical. In order to materialize this view, what should we do? What I have been talking about so far constitutes my efforts to tackle these issues.

The land or the earth is not an issue that must be tied to an old-fashioned or a tradition-affiliated way of thinking. I think it is possible to pave the way to a new vista, if we bring to light the Buddhist view of "the corrupt and vile world *sive* the Pure Land," by connecting it with the historical world of Buddhist truth. What Buddhists thought in ancient times of the dictum "the corrupt and vile world *sive* the Pure Land" remains unclear. But I think it necessary to reconsider this view in a new light. I think that there is some possibility of our being able to give it another shape than the old-fashioned meaning imbedded in the dichotomy of spiritualism and idealism. We also need to inquire into the meaning of the Buddhist dictum that the bodhisattvas sprang forth from the ground.

Part Two

On the Modernization of Buddhism

3

What Is Modernization?

The Historical Character of a Human Being

I have had the opportunity to say something about Buddhism at the Association of the Great Earth before. I am afraid that my talk this time may be concerned with the same topic. Mention is often made of modernization. I took notice of the phrase *monpō* (to listen to Buddha's truth) written on a signboard in this meeting room. An attempt to talk about the modernization of Buddhism will deviate somewhat from this *monpō*, understood in the traditional sense. Rather, what I have in mind in terms of the modernization of Buddhism is a problem that should be argued from a perspective prior to *monpō*. It is concerned with the problem of what attitude is demanded of listeners when *monpō* is the point at issue. Even though this problem is prior to *monpō*, I am convinced that it is a problem having to do with the essence of *monpō*. That is to say, if this problem is left unsolved, then for us *monpō* will remain out of our reach. If so, we may fall victim to the scratching of our itching foot through our shoes, thereby yielding little in spite of many efforts to tackle *monpō*. What is the problem to be dealt with prior to *monpō*? In a word, it does not make sense to take modernization into account without having recourse to tradition. But at the same time, to ponder the possibilities of modernization only within the framework of tradition is of no avail, nor will it enable us to truly vitalize the meaning of tradition. Briefly speaking, my view is that we cannot genuinely tackle tradition except in the process of its coming into contact with the modern world in one form or another, and that if we try to come to understand the modern world in connection with the background of history, then tradition is inevitably called into question. The problem under consideration is intimately connected with the historical existence of a human being—that is to say, with the historical structure of human existence. In this sense, it is the most

71

basic problem of *monpō*. Because of this, it seems to be a difficult problem to cope with. To speak the truth, I cannot get rid of the feeling that I, who am too old to speak of modernization without thereby becoming perplexed, am not in a position to deal with it, and perhaps it is more appropriate for younger people to ponder it, and to speak of it in various ways, so that it is rather I who must stand on the side of *monpō*. We old persons should be in a position to listen to *monpō*. This happens all the time in other situations. Young people tend to be daring in speaking of something without hesitation, even though their views must be based upon something firm. Since there is in youthfulness that which refuses to be confined to the past, it is of no use that we try to prevent the young from exercising force of a kind akin to a bamboo sprout springing up through the ground. Even if there are stones, it springs up besides them obliquely. I am sure that young people's boldness inevitably will make the issue of modernization acute, in the true sense of the word. In former days, I had an occasion to speak of this problem in general terms. So this time, I would like to deal with it by avoiding duplication as much as possible.

The Historical and the Suprahistorical

I would like to talk about modernization, not in its ambiguous form but in connection with the above-mentioned problem of human existence, while giving heed to the historical characteristics of the latter, at least to some extent. I think that faith gives us a clue concerning where we should begin to deal with this problem of human existence. It is generally held that faith is the most basic concern for religions such as Buddhism and Christianity. But faith is something not only concerned with religion but also already associated with our daily life. So I would like to set the starting point of our argument at our daily life, and then to inquire into the significance that faith has here, and how it comes to be connected with the religious dimension. One question to be raised here is how we are inevitably led to religious faith if we pursue matters of our daily life to their logical consequence, that is, if we carry on the search for truth. Religious truth is understood to be concerned with something eternal and unchangeable, and its characteristic feature can be described in terms of permanent laws or dharma. In this way, we must carry on our search, for faith involves something basically unchangeable. Various things occur in the neighborhood of a human being. And no sooner has he or she tried to search for something true about them than they give rise to new problems, one after another. In spite of this, he or she makes every effort to glean something permanent from this turmoil of problems occasioned in the search for truth. The point is that what is eternal and unchangeable has the authentic feature of being just as it is, irrespective of how a human being may think or deal with it.

Even though we may return to the eternal as the authentically unchangeable, nonetheless it comes to be affiliated with the stream of time that is familiar in our daily life as constantly moving, and so we submit it to various sorts of reexamination. That is to say, the reexamination of what was once grasped, and has since been transmitted as something unchangeable—my view is that the unchangeable is above all based upon tradition—seems to take place here. Since constant change occurs on the part of time, something unchangeable makes its appearance, it seems to me, under the guise of activities that proceed to accommodate themselves to the transition of time, so that it goes on creating or constructing something novel and imparting new structure to what flows, without definite end.

If the term "accommodate" implies that the unchangeable caters to the stream of time, then it terminates in a loss of its character as unchangeable truth. But if truth has a vitality, as I assume it has, then I think that it must be provided with the capacity to impart a structure to what undergoes constant change without thereby keeping aloof from the latter. Here some very difficult problems arise. It has often been repeated that unchangeableness and fashionableness must be made into one. This is also perhaps the fundamental standpoint of Buddhism. I am convinced that this is in essence what is meant by the phrase "a twofold truth of the sacred-secular." This is also exactly the characteristic of history that is now at issue among scholars. It seems to me that the assumption that historicity is made possible on the ground of these two sides—that is, unchangeableness and fashionableness—was set forth recently by scholars in comparatively clear-cut form. In my view, it is the standpoint of Christian theology in particular that has brought this assumption to expression very clearly. On the basis of K. Barth's dialectical theology, R. Bultmann and Christian theology subsequent to him seem to have tried to probe into this problem quite thoroughly. We can say that this is due to the fact that Christianity is, in its origin, a religion with historical characteristics. But apart from this, we can also say that religion, of whatever sort it may be, cannot be rendered active without having these two sides, in one way or another.

The Authentic Structure of History

What does the term "historical" mean? In particular, in what sense does the theology now under investigation use it? In German-speaking areas where theology of this sort is now in vogue, there is a German word that is equivalent to history, *Geschichte*, and that is to be distinguished from *Historie*. The latter originally means to talk about stories or to hand down legends. But it is often pointed out that the former is derived from the verb *geschehen*, which indicates that something happens or that something novel that has never been before has arisen. We are able to describe such a thing by means of English words such as "occur," "happen" or "event." Hence the term "historical" is not adequate to cope with this. Here human existence itself appears on the scene as essentially having historical characteristics. In other words, in the midst of the fact that some new things now constantly come to arise, human existence is also established. So far as the term *Historie* is concerned, it consists in tracing back to past events by looking back on them from the present. This is the case with those who are usually called historians. It is a matter of great concern for learning to pursue and investigate events, teachings, and thoughts in the past. Even if we are concerned with the present, by reason of the fact that it is based upon the past it is necessary for us to make the effort to clarify and to precisely comprehend the past. While this business is something with which historians have to be engaged, problems of history are so complicated that, if we make a thorough investigation of what truly happened in the past, we cannot help but confront those who really managed to live in those days, and come to grips with the issue of what they really thought about and looked after. This means that the problem of history terminates in the problem of what is going on inside a human being. The inside of a human being refers to that quality of human existence by virtue of which a human being is truly a human being. In contast, by the term "outside" I have in mind matters such as economics and politics. Particularly in the case of economics, rather than politics, human existence retreats into the background, and in its place, topics such as the structure of external relations between human beings—social structures, social organizations, and so forth—come to increase in importance. We can say even with respect to economics that, since it is burdened with a human being's desires, it cannot be thought of apart from a human being. But it can be acknowledged that it is, generally speaking, a little bit removed from the internal concerns of a human being, such as issues of culture or mind.

Therefore, history, if we pursue it to its consequences and confront the issue of a human being, terminates in what a person looks for, that is, the culture of mind. As a result, a historian who engages himself or herself in describing past histories is gradually required to identify himself or herself with persons in the past, and to embark upon a detailed investigation of the interior problems of what kinds of issues they were really concerned with. If so, even though we are concerned here with matters of fact in the past, we cannot simply dismiss them as bygones. In order to understand them, we are required to make ourselves contemporaneous with the past.

In this way I think that a historian's task is gradually transformed from the standpoint of *Historie* (that is, of a mere description of the past) to that of an interior human understanding of events (that is, of *Geschehen*). The present and the past, even though they differ with respect to their period, thereby come to be connected with each other. It is often remarked that the past and the present are contemporary with each other. What is opened up here is the standpoint that is called simultaneousness, in which the past and the present are said to be contemporary, while the past is still the past and the present is still the present. This becomes true, if we confine our argument to an inquiry into the term "history." And judging from the standpoint of present actuality, we can say that a connection with the past is a basic necessity, as is clear from the foregoing argument. I hold the view that this aspect of connection consists in contemporaneousness in the final analysis.

So it turns out that we understand the present in such a way that what people in the past looked for is tied up with what we are looking for in the present. It is only on the basis of this contemporaneousness that the present genuinely comes to be connected with the past. It is only then that we can say that the past combines with the present and that the present combines with the past by our stepping back toward it.

This can be said only because the present looks for something— that is to say, it aims at the future with its eye looking forward, without thereby being satisfied with reliance on the past. In this case, the present really makes its appearance as the present, instead of as the past. This means that in events authentically active in the present, there is involved a forward-looking direction, which has the future in view as its most basic element. This fact we can describe either as the present aiming at the future, or as the latter casting its shadow on the former. It is necessary for us to determine our attitude or to set forth our existence in the present, over which the future casts its shadow at all times.

For this reason, to be able truly to go back to the past means that we go back from the present and open up the standpoint of contemporaneousness with the past, and that the present turns out truly to be the present. The view that the present turns out truly to be the present indicates that it achieves independence from the past in a sense—the phrase "in a sense" refers to a relative independence. But to be independent of the past is, conversely, established at one and the same time as our endeavor to decidedly meet a call from the future—this call means nothing else than that a new problem is now taking place—as a current issue that must concern us. Roughly speaking, contemporaneousness is a domain in which two things happen simultaneously—that is, the domain in which the past heads for the future, on the one hand, and the future heads for the past and is investigated by thereby being illuminated, on the other hand. Thus, the future cannot be authentically probed without a deep understanding of the past. A unilateral stream of time from the past to the present and from the present to the future is here of no avail. Rather, what is now under consideration are two distinct points: one is that the future is turned around in the present, back to the past with the present as a center, and that various problems that are now happening in connection with the future come to be illuminated in the light of the past in the midst of their being affiliated with the latter; and the other is that the past gains illumination from the light of the future. This latter point has to do with the question of how the traditions of the past come to be activated in the present. I think that the present is a domain in which these two sides move as one, and come to be established through an interweaving of each another.

My point is that basically human existence has an historical character in this sense. When a human being is said to exist here and now, two streams of time, from the past to the future and from the future to the past, combine through the medium of the present to become one in the present of human existence. It sounds a little bit fantastic to make mention of the stream of time as flowing from the future to the past. This we cannot avoid, if we are to adequately take account of time.

A Human's Faithfulness and Trustworthiness

Now, let it be supposed that a human being is as has just been described. Then a question must be posed as to what faith in the world is like. As was asserted before, this is a matter of basic concern for various religions, including Buddhism and Christianity. In most cases, it is accounted for in terms of the relationship between God or Buddha and a human being. But before that, it must be dealt with in and through the relationship between one human being and another, even though we are well advised, I am sure, not to be content only with the latter relationship, if we push the matter a little bit further.

One of the most urgent problems facing a human being in the present world is that in the relationships between human beings, for the basis on which these relationships are established is in the process of disappearing. To speak straightforwardly, it becomes more and more difficult to cope with the problem of where in the world human reliability is still found. This is the issue of the mutual trust of human beings. I do not think it necessary to probe deeply into this problem. But in the final analysis, man's faithfulness or truthfulness, as it is often referred to in Confucianism, is the crucial issue. Confucianism points out from early on, especially in the book entitled *Chung yung,* that the heart and soul of a human being are affiliated at their basis with a somewhat religious dimension. In this book, truthfulness is regarded as the way of heaven. This seems to be equivalent to the view that truthfulness is a human being's innate disposition. Behind this view lies a way of thinking that assumes that it is the practice of human beings that makes this innate disposition truly trustworthy.

The point at issue is a human being's truthfulness, by virtue of which the relation between human beings is rendered trustworthy from beginning to end. That we can trust each other through and through means that we can by no means be deceived in our human relations, no matter what accidents may occur. Therefore, we can say that a human relation cannot truly be a relation between one human being and another, unless it involves within itself the fact of being trustworthy. In the event that we come to fear that a friend of ours deceives us by reason of his ego-centered motives, such as self-interest or pleasure, we cannot have a genuine friendship with him or her, however intimate our relationship may be. A prerequisite for genuine friendship is the trust that he or she by no means deceives us, what- ever may happen. A further requisite in this case is that the certainty that we have in his or her trustworthiness must in turn be transmitted inside us, and vice versa. Simply speaking, it must be that each human being possesses such certainty of trustworthy existence, that is, truth- fulness within himself or herself. Let us assume here that there are two persons called A and B, respectively. Thus, even though B is subject to severe criticism from society on suspicion of faults or er- rors—he cannot avoid making errors, because he is a human being— A does not waiver in his trust in B nor have any doubt of B, so far as the basis of their mutual friendship is concerned. This is because A has a certainty about B's trustworthiness and B does not deceive A in

his relations or attitudes toward him. This means that A and B have
a clear sense of trustworthiness with respect to each other by virtue of
which they are able to establish a mutual reliance. That A assumes
trustworthiness on B's part renders it possible for B to be sure that A
can rely on him. In this way, a mutual trustworthiness is established,
which involves a relation of pledging, that is, *engagement*, to use a
French expression. Here a sort of promise is involved, but the connection between the two persons is more internalized than in an ordinary
relation. We Japanese once spoke of *en* (ties). What we have in mind
with this word is not simply an accidental connection, but something
that we cannot dispose of merely by appealing to the authentically
accidental even though it occurred accidentally. This word denotes
something accidental and at the same time something not accidental,
the essential feature of which we Japanese describe in the phrase: "We
are destined from the previous life to have this or that relation." It is
said that even a chance meeting is due to the karma of a previous life,
and in that relationship in which a man and a woman marry due to
en, there seems to be a fundamental tie involved between the one
human existence and the other.

En may be a word derived from Buddhism. But this word is not
confined to Buddhism, but applies to the existence of a human being
in general. I am sure that a wedding ceremony in a shrine, as has been
performed in Japan from ancient times, is likely to give expression to
this authentic meaning. It is not enough to say that we marry by
entering into a contract by our own free will, as sometimes happens
at present. It goes without saying, however, that the will is also required. But the will alone does not render a marriage capable of being
necessary. It is not simply that a man and a woman just happen to see
each other, and then come to be married. Instead, the genuine connection between one human being and another is in need of some perma-
nency by virtue of which it will not, basically speaking, undergo any
change. This is the reason why a wedding ceremony is performed
before God. In this case, the phrase "before God" designates a place
where human beings make a promise by returning to the ground of
their being from which to obtain their conjugal ties. The phrase "ground
of being" here refers to the fact that one human being and another are
tied to each other through getting back to an opened-up place that is
said to exist before God. I think that what is at stake here is the contract or promise that they make with a view to uniting with each other
by returning to a kind of disclosure that exists at the ground of being;
it is a return to the most basic place from which beings, of whatever
sort they may be, come to *geschehen*. If we go as far as this, then it

implies religious significance. But the point at issue here is rather with the trustworthiness of a human being who appears on the scene there, with which social ethics, but not religion, so to speak, is concerned. However this may be, I am convinced that this sort of trustworthiness of a human being must be the foundation of a marriage.

I maintain the view that trust in others is united with a certainty that one possesses concerning oneself—that is, a self-reliance. It contains within itself the determination and the certainty about oneself that cause others not to deceive. Here trust in others and self-reliance are united as one. If it is the case that we only rely on ourselves, then this reliance is a self-reliance in the ordinary sense, but is likely to terminate in self-complacency or excessive self-confidence. Instead, only when trust in others obtains as being at one with one's being able to truly rely on others is it possible for one's connection with others to be truly established. What is involved here is the view that trust in others includes within itself a sort of open-mindedness that is accepting of oneself and at the same time of others, and that one includes within oneself a sort of disclosed mind of a kind that can render others capable of living authentically as others.

To use terminology characteristic of Buddhism, what is now at issue is nonselfhood; it is a disclosure—that is, an open-mindedness—that can be appropriately described in terms of other-centeredness instead of ego-centeredness. Therefore, even though self-confidence is here spoken of, it is not ego-centered. Nevertheless, there is something certain within one. This is nothing else than a subjectivity whose essential feature is characterized by means of "no-selfhood." While it is subjective, it has at the same time a broadness of mind that can accept others just as they are—or, to say it another way, to make others be what they are. This is why Japanese people, in ancient times, used to speak of no-selfhood or the nonduality of oneself and the other.

The trustworthiness of a human being consists in holding trust at the place where no-selfhood obtains. Here a human being's truthfulness is also included. But in this case, the term "human being" is meant to refer to the relationship between one human being and another. While the relationship between oneself and the other is here spoken of, however, each of them is at the same time subjective in the genuine sense of the word. This means that each of them is just what he or she is. In the fact that A and B have respectively their own certainty that A is A and B is B, it occurs that A enables B to be activated in himself or herself. We are able to describe this way of being in terms of a "no-selfhood-like subjectivity." This is nothing else than what is described in terms of the phrase the "nonduality of oneself and the other." In other words, the fact that A is truly A himself or herself makes it possible that B is truly B himself or herself.

It is only through this that trustworthiness comes to arise. Because of this, trustworthiness consists in one's holding one's trust in others in and through the relationship between oneself and others. What I want to say here is that one's self-reliance comes to be established in the midst of one's having trust in others on the basis of this nonduality of oneself and the other.

The I-Thou Relationship

However this may be, the situation referred to as the alienation of a human being stands in the way, so that the above-mentioned relationship is unlikely to be realized. This situation constitutes one of the basic issues confronting a human being in the contemporary world. It prevents an authentic human relationship from arising. As a consequence, the place in which each human being is enabled truly to be who he or she is of his or her own accord is not yet opened up.

Normally, this kind of issue is discussed under the theme of "I and thou." The theme indicates that it is only through accepting the other truly as "thou" that I am also able to become "I" in the true sense of the word. It is only through taking you for granted as the subject called "thou" that I am likely to become a subject myself.

Then the question must be posed as to what this place of being is like. This is a philosophical question, even though a number of problems come to arise in this connection. Within Mahāyāna Buddhism, philosophical arguments intervened in the San-lun, Consciousness-Only, and the Tiantai schools, which had developed in scope in their expansion from India to China. Even though mention was made of philosophical arguments, they differ in kind from philosophies that are in vogue in the Western world, since they are concerned with thoughts of the Middle Path inherent in Buddhism. Nevertheless, we can say that philosophical problems carry weight here.

For instance, philosophical questions such as those concerned with being and nothingness are now dealt with under the title of ontology, which seem to be among the central issues even in Western philosophies. I have no intention, however, of elaborating on this problem now. I would rather like to consider a human being's being, which we can take account of as the way in which a human being originates as a being. In this case, we must consider what a human being's being is like. The essential feature characteristic of a being called "human" appears here under the guise of "I am," which is different from the dictum that a desk is or a pine tree is. In other words, each human being has a way of being as an individual subject. The term "I" has a strong tendency to refer to those characteristics that are unique to each human being, those which are hidden and not liable to be understood by others. This means, fundamentally speaking, that in a human being there is something hidden.

This holds true with respect to various other things in our daily life as well. For instance, sensations such as seeing and hearing involve something that nobody can know except the person concerned, as has been said since ancient times through such phrases as "For us to know whether it is cool or warm can be achieved only by ourselves." We cannot know whether water is hot or not until we really come to drink it. In the final analysis, knowledge of this sort is understood to be affiliated with the human body, with which "I am" is also tied. For this reason, we cannot deal with the human body in the same way as we do with other physical bodies. Even in cases of other "sentient beings," as referred to in Buddhism, the body still seems to be called into question. The reason why it is not dealt with as merely a physical body is that it brings to expression being itself. So far as a human being is concerned, the body is just this human being.

For example, let us consider an accident in which someone beats me up. This occurrence cannot be exhaustively described by appealing merely to the physical phenomenon that one physical body clashes with another. Instead, the fact is that it is you who beat me. In this case, the partner becomes "thou" instead of merely a physical body. There arises the relationship between I and thou.

Supposing that a human body is merely physical, then it is only an object of physics, but this is not the case with a human being. Because of this, the character of "I" and "thou" is revealed in the way of being as a body. But at the same time, the latter has two aspects, because it is also a physical body. Human beings appear to each other in the form of a human body. Abstracting from this, we are able to regard them as merely physical bodies. It is of great importance that they appear to each other in the form of a human body by virtue of which each of them is enabled to have his or her own partner. Since what is at stake here is the fact that each of them comes to arise as a human body and makes himself or herself appear to the other, we may be allowed to describe this fact in terms of the place of relationship in the ontological sense.

But so far as the phrase "a human body is" is concerned, judging from the aspect in which it is tied up with "I am," we can say that it appears on the scene and at the same time withdraws from this appearance. While it appears in the form of a human body, it has, basically speaking, something that refuses to appear, so far as the aspect of "I am" is concerned. This means that it is affiliated with such bodily functions as hearing and seeing, on the one hand, and that these physical functions are also tied up with the mind, on the other. This also means that the fact that a human body comes to arise cannot be accounted for in separation from the mind. With respect to this latter aspect, there is something at its basis to which no one else has access, except the person concerned.

The reason why this can be said is that the person concerned is an individual in the sense that he or she absolutely exists by himself or herself. This is manifest in the human body. Because of this, the relationship between oneself and the other through which it occurs that you beat me comes to be realized by the human body. By "realize" I mean that a human being appears on the scene while leaving something hidden behind himself or herself to the very end. With something truly hidden, he or she discloses himself or herself to others. One will disappear, if one does not possess something hidden. In a human being is involved something contradictory such that one discloses oneself while being in possession of something that one can by no means disclose. Otherwise, we cannot say that a human relationship between oneself and the other is, nevertheless, established as an I-thou relationship, while appearing on the scene under the guise of the human body.

The problem I have just mentioned about human relations arises in connection with the human body. But fundamentally speaking, it cannot be called into question apart from the contention that each of the persons constituting this relation is subjective—or rather, I should say, an individual.

It is by keeping the above-mentioned points in mind that the problem of whether or not we trust others seems to be posed in the case of a human being.

A Human's Subjectivity and the Issue of the Human Body

I will now try to make the problem of the human body clear, since otherwise something remains unexplained.

It is often remarked that trustworthiness plays an important role in human relations, and that the loss of it gives rise to the alienation of a human being. The question is: why are we deprived of trustworthiness, or what is the cause of the undermining of human relations?

In connection with these issues, a further question is posed as to how to deal with a human being. In an attempt to grapple with these questions, I discussed the issue of the human body in the preceding section. But at the same time, what I intended to do there was to make it clear that being and its place cannot be separated from each other.

Mention was already made of a "disclosure." To turn to the topic now in question, the issue of being concerning an individual human being cannot be accounted for apart from the betweenness, or the relation, that he or she bears to other human beings. This sort of affair is involved in the issue of the I-thou relationship, where what is at stake is the problem concerning being and its place. This issue of place has to do with a disclosure. Our being has its own place, which is in this case designated in terms of "togetherness," and in which we appear on the scene together with others. It is in the place of being that this "togetherness" arises. A genuine "togetherness" cannot be established unless we truly become ourselves.

In human relations such as that of parent and child, husband and wife, or a lord and vassals, there is something involved that, in one way or another, can be described in terms of friendship. We cannot clarify the relation between a parent and a child without having recourse to the friendship involved there, by virtue of which one human being and another can live together. In the Japanese syllable *ho* in *dōbō*, the meaning is almost equivalent to "brothers" or "fellow human beings," and the term "together" refers to the basic structure inherent in a human being, according to which he or she is absolutely individualized and at the same time connected with "togetherness." At first sight, these two aspects seem to be contradictory. But apart from them, a human being cannot come to be established. This fact is ordinarily conceived of as something contradictory, because one takes a discursive standpoint. However, my point is to consider what the basic structure of a human being is like.

The contention that being cannot be separated from its place indicates that the character of place intervenes in the structure of being. If we confine our argument to what we have been concerned with so far, we must ask the question: what is the indicator that informs us that the relation between one person and another has come to be? This can be conceived in various ways. So far as ethics is concerned, I am sure that, fundamentally speaking, it terminates in the issue of mind—that is to say, in a subjective way of being a human being. In addition, the question must be raised as to what this place is like, in which one subjective agent and another come to meet each other and to live together, and how such subjective ways of being are made possible. In my opinion, this sense of place differs greatly from the notion of place usually conceived of. By the term "place" we usually imagine something spacelike, something extended. But the place now in question has, according to my view, the characteristic of a disclosure of mind that comes to manifest itself in each person's mind. That is to say, it is the place wherein one person (A) and another (B) reflect each other in such a fashion that A discloses within herself a place in which B is enabled to be B, and conversely B discloses within herself a place in which A is enabled to be A. In order for this state of affairs to be possible, I think that the place itself must possess a subjective quality. It seems to me that this is precisely what is described in terms of "mind." Place has the characteristic of mind, and conversely, the mind involves within itself the characteristic of place. One thing to be noted, however, is that the mind is, I think, tied up with the human body.

The issue of the basic place consists in asserting that the human body is meant to refer to the person concerned. It is a human body all right, but at the same time, it has the characteristic of being the particular person concerned. This idea is very important. But I would like to leave it for another occasion. What I want to emphasize here is that the place of being has the quality of land. To use terms characteristic of Buddhism, it is also brought to expression by means of the "Land of the Buddhas," which is almost equivalent to the "Kingdom of God" in Christianity.

The concept of the "Land of the Buddhas" or of the land of a country indicates an essential connection between the body and the land. Keeping an eye on the phrase "the body of the Buddha," it must be that the Buddha and his land are conceived of as incapable of being separated from each other after all. The being of the Buddha and his land are associated with each other. It is said that when a bodhisattva becomes a Buddha, he will establish his own land in certain circumstances. It is here that the issue of land arises where the Buddha is essentially established as the Buddha. If we advance this argument further by including sentient beings by standing on that foundation in which religion originates, we can say that it is here that the being of a human being takes possession of its place. By the term "place" I mean that in which one person and another come to associate themselves with each other. It also involves within itself the meaning of land. (To use the term "relation" here, instead of "associate," seems not to be appropriate, because it is likely to lead us to think that individuals are presupposed and then afterward come to enter into relations with each other. If one sticks to the use of the term "relation," it should imply that it is more important than each of the individuals. Instead of the view that individuals are presupposed and that the relation between them then comes to arise, what I have here in mind is that relation which individuals bear to each other, and without which each individual cannot render himself or herself capable of being established.)

The Issue of the Human Body and that of the Mind

What we are basically concerned with here is the issue of mind. At the same time, the human body must be called into question. So I think it necessary to say that we must deal with the issue of body and mind in their unity. Since consideration of either mind or body leaves something not yet clarified, we need to subject them both to further investigation. While it is necessary for us to inquire into what a human being is in terms of the unity of mind and body, the issue of land thereby comes to surface. Then, in connection with this, a number of topics come into view—for example, society, a household, a state, etc.— all of which leave something unclarified. Besides this, that society which is neither a household nor a state is also called into question.

In spheres such as theory, the social sciences, or sociology, a distinction has been made of old with regard to a household or a state— that is, between *Gemeinschaft* and *Gesellschaft*. This distinction seems to be of great importance. Various phenomena such as the disintegration of a family, the severance of the parent-child relation, and a conflict between husband and wife are found as manifestations of human alienation. But behind them lies the deterioration of relations between the members of a family due to the fact that they are deprived of mutual trust. In addition, there is an increasing tendency among people not to pay due heed to the notion of the state. On the contrary, a society, but not a state, is to be brought out in full relief as something to be dealt with. What is the reason for this?

The term "society" is here employed in a broad sense inclusive of a whole, in just the same way that social science or sociology use it. But in its narrow sense, it is the connection between individuals provided with basic human rights, as is not the case with a family or a state; in this case, their absolute subjectivity is represented by the basic human rights with which they are provided. And these connections between individuals appear there in the form of contracts. Here the issues relating to the family or the state might be left out of account. This fact, that contracts have replaced connections between individuals, seems to have originated under the circumstance that the social sciences arose in a way in which a scientific way of thinking has predominated. But what I have in mind here is the problem of whether or not we can have a perspective that is a little different from that.

For instance, when we inquire into the human body, there is certainly the possibility of treating it only as a physical body, as something materialistic. But without reaching such an abstraction, it is important to think in such a way that a human relation cannot be accounted for apart from the human body, and that the relations concerned with the human body are nothing else than human relations. Otherwise, we cannot make clear the fact that parents are related to their children by blood, and that the conjugal relations between husband and wife are at once constitutive of human relations. If we assume that individuals are presupposed and then are brought into relation with each other, the content of this relation is thought to be composed of rights such as are called basic human rights; then I have the impression that the relation between parents and children as well as between husband and wife are basically nullified by these assumptions. A scientific way of thinking is of this sort, roughly speaking. But I wonder if it is possible for us to take a slightly different view.

This possibility has to do with the issue of the human body, on the one hand, and that of the mind in connection with the body, on the other. Furthermore, it has to do with the problem of the land regarded as the place wherein human beings, with body and mind, are related to each other. When we give an account of the nature of a state or a family, I am certain that they will be shown to have been brought into connection with the land. In line with this view, religious human relations arise. The reason why such notions as the Land of the Buddhas and the Kingdom of God have arisen is because of the fact that the being of a human being itself implies the land of the country, which is regarded as the place wherein a human body, mind, and land are all taken into account. Is it not possible for us to probe a little further into these topics, which have to do with the question of the Pure Land in Buddhism?

The Buddhist Dictum that "All sentient beings are in possession of Buddha Nature"

Human relations are ordinarily conceived of as ethical issues. In order that they may be authentically provided with certainty, it is inevitable that they be based on truthfulness. Otherwise, mutual trustworthiness does not arise. Here the term "trustworthiness" is meant to refer to something unchangeable in the midst of transient human relations. By the phrase "something unchangeable" I mean that, even though human beings perish one after another, the relationship of friendship or the mutual trust that obtained between them remained intact. We can go as far as to say that it occurs only at the place where the stream of time is transcended. It has been said that the term "Buddha-nature" indicates in sentient beings—that is, in human beings— that something unchangeable is involved. I am convinced that when people focus on this point they come to speak of "Buddha-nature." In the *Nirvāna Sūtra* it is remarked that "All sentient beings are in possession of a Buddha-nature without exception." Even though it may be possible to interpret this phrase in various ways, we tend to accept an ordinary interpretation according to which all sentient beings are provided with a Buddha-nature. And what is more, it is also said that Tathāgatas are everlasting and undergo no change. There is here a place where the changeable and the unchangeable intersect. And in this intersection, a Buddha-nature is thought to arise. On the one hand, it is often remarked that Buddha-nature has a quality such as is disclosed by the statement that Tathāgatas are everlasting, and, on the other, it is remarked that it is to be found in all sentient beings. Then what in the world does the phrase "all are" in the sentence "All are in possession of" mean? It sometimes induces us to a somewhat superficial grasp of its meaning. But what does it mean that there is a Buddha-nature, or that all are in possession of Buddha-nature? By pushing these statements to their logical consequence, Dōgen drew the unique conclusion that " 'all are' refers to nothing else but the Buddha-nature." Then in what way does the Pure Land sect of Buddhism think of this matter? I am sure that such issues as *kihō* (this Japanese word implies two things: the minds of sentient beings believing in Buddha, and the Buddha's power to bring this belief into realization) and the practice of the invocation of Amida Buddha are derived from the "being" in "all are."

I think that from this problem of Buddha-nature is derived the problem of "land," as well as the being of sentient beings and its place. As far as the statement that "All sentient beings are in possession of Buddha-nature" is concerned, the term "Buddha-nature" and "all are" are liable to be conceived in various ways. But apart from "Buddha-nature," a genuine human environment could not be established. In resolving the issue of whether human beings are trustworthy, or are truthful of each other, we cannot dispose of the matter simply by appealing to human affairs, but the "Buddha-nature" must thereby be accounted for. This Buddha-nature is conceived of in the

direction of the subjectivity of nonselfhood. It is conceived of as subjective, while being nonselfhood to the very end, and it is also conceived of as nonselfhood, while being subjective through and through.
My point is to ask whether or not there is any possibility of conceiving
of the issue of land on the basis of Buddha-nature. Buddhism main-
tains the view that "Buddha-nature is at once Tathāgata," or that "a
great trust is Buddha-nature." Trust cannot, after all, be conceived of
apart from the subjectivity of a human being. In this case, the problem
of subjectivity cannot be dealt with exhaustively in terms of subjectivity regarded as self-power alone. Fundamentally speaking, I also think
that it is dealt with as accompanying the quality of other-power.

However this may be, I ask whether or not there is the possibility of
inquiring a bit deeper into the issue of the land, if we proceed to think
of the matter in compliance with Shinran's standpoint that "a great trust
is Buddha-nature," or that "Buddha-nature is at once Tathāgata."

With regard to the Pure Land, it is not that we conceive of it as
something fantastically far away from us. It certainly differs absolutely from this impure world. But I hold the view that precisely this
absolute difference renders it possible for this impure world to be
established. We must also consider what it means for us to be delivered or not. Although the Pure Land and the impure world are divided into two on the boundary line within which one assures oneself
that peace of mind obtains, they are connected with each other somewhere. Therefore, we can say that they are two, and at the same time
are united into one. Apart from this unity, we could not afford to speak
of the impure world and of the Pure Land as well. We can say that
purity and impurity are connected to the effect that they reflect on each
other. My point is to ask whether or not it is possible for us to give an
account of a human being by standing on this interconnection.

So far as modernization is concerned, in the case of Buddhism I
think it necessary to take into consideration the issue of being and its
place, or rather (to use terminology peculiar to Buddhism), the issue
of the Land of the Buddhas or the Pure Land. We cannot deal with the
problem of modernization only by being engaged in mere renovation.
Instead, I am certain that the issue of modernization leads us to inquire into the problem of where the meaning of the Pure Land, for
instance, makes its appearance in a form that is pregnant with significance for us, by bringing it into confrontation with the problems of the
modern world.

4

A Departure from the "Individual"

A Human Existence

Yesterday, I began by attempting to deal with the relationship that ordinarily holds between "I and thou," that is, the relationship between subject and subject. My aim was to clarify the sorts of problems that are involved in this relationship. Human existence can be characterized as being absolutely alone—that is to say, as not being substitutable by any other. This is precisely what is meant by an individual, in the genuine sense of the word. In order to describe what it is, the term "the single one" is sometimes used in the Western world. It was Kierkegaard who first made use of it. By placing emphasis on existence or subjectivity, he asserted that existence is nothing but the standpoint of subjectivity. Although such words as "existence" and "subjectivity" had circulated widely as familiar words, he imparted to them quite a different meaning from that which they had originally possessed. For instance, even in Japan, the equivalent word for existence has long been used in the sense of real entities existing in the actual world. But what happens if we push the fact that these entities exist in the actual world to its logical conclusion? Perhaps we come to conclude that the way of being according to which they are each pure entities that are not interchangeable with others is their real way of being in the world. And it is only in a human being that this real way of being as an individual is most genuinely and explicitly revealed.

Since ancient times, everyone has known that what exists in the real world are individual existences, a theme that has been dealt with philosophically since Plato and Aristotle. The problem is to ask what characteristics may be applied to "to be." Two things are to be noted here. On the one hand, what is in the actual world possesses the characteristic of singularity or individuality. On the other, it also has universality. According to the latter, there is no entity that exists only as a mere individual, rather, individuals, whatever they may be, always exist in such a way as to be susceptible to asking the question of what they are. That they exist in this way means that they exist in such a way as to answer that they are such and such. For instance, the answer may be that they are desks, or papers, or human beings. When we say that something is "this" or "that," we pinpoint particular individuals. But, when we say that they are human beings or desks, we denote not only particular individuals, but also that which cannot be confined to particular individuals, and whose number cannot be exhaustively enumerated. There is an indefinite number of human beings, for example. The same can be said of desks, which also cannot be confined to particular existents alone. It is noteworthy here that beings have these two aspects. This knowledge has to do with the basic principles in accordance with which we think of things.

For instance, when *A* is said to be *B*, we used to say that *S* is *P*, because *A* is the subject, and *B* is the predicate. This is a judgment. And a judgment is the basis through which we subject things to our thinking. As to judgment, when asked what something is, we answer that it is such and such. In this case, "this" indicates an individual, and a predicate denoted in terms of "such and such" is a universal. In answering the question in what manner the "is" is established in the statement that a thing is, the important thing to take note of is the fact that it is established on the basis of the relationship between individuality and universality. It can be said that logic brings to expression a judgment as a basic form of our thinking, as we proceed to think of things. Seen from one angle, it can be said to be a form by means of which we manage to think of things. At the same time, it opens up what is, or it discloses its "being" by subjecting it to analysis. Its job is to open up a thing so as to designate it as such and such. In this way, the structure of being, which consists of the connection between individuality and universality, is brought to light. What is disclosed here is the structure of being such that something individual is at the same time universal.

In other words, the basic form of logic at once opens up the structure of being, and at the same time is the basic form through which we think of things. We can say that logic is that in which a thinking agent, and something thought—that is, a subject and an object—come into contact with each other as that which discloses both of them simultaneously. Here logic—that is, reason—has to do with the issue of our thinking as well as of that of being. In the Western world, there is the word *logos*. It signifies the law of the being of things and, at the same time, it has various other meanings, such as the laws of thinking, of judgment, of logic, or of language. It has the same meaning as *ri* or *rihō* in Japanese—that is, the rational law as spoken of in the East. Here the term *rihō* involves thinking or speaking. I have the impression that it is somewhat equivalent to the Japanese word *nori*, which means a law and at the same time involves starting to talk. Yet even here individuality is called into question, while it also takes on the form of universality. Here is the form of a being according to which it is predicated as having a universal form, such as that of a desk or a pine tree. Therefore, an individual and a universal form are assumed to be united.

However this may be, when Kierkegaard speaks of "the single one," he intends to go beyond the view according to which individuality is said to be universality. We wonder if we are able to grasp the real feature of things, that is, the authentic being of their really existing in the actual world, insofar as we try to see them by taking the viewpoint of what is called "reason," or of discursive thinking. This is because this viewpoint consists in seeing things from the standpoint of universality through and through, by transferring them to the level of reason. Instead, if we go so far as authentic reality, then by pushing our argument to its logical consequence, we must ponder things by participating in the place where an individual exists as an individual, by taking leave of reason. The view that individuality is universality is of great importance, and it consists in our having knowledge of something. But what I want to assert is that unless we get beyond this paradigm, we cannot think of genuine reality. Once we take our stand on genuine reality, it is clearly disclosed that an individual is not universal but individual—namely, that it has the characteristic of being irreplaceable by anything else. It is in a human being that this characteristic is revealed most conspicuously. The phrase "I am" gives expression to this characteristic. It can be said that this phrase expresses a human being's way of being, which is based upon his or her absolute individuality—that is, on the most real feature of his or her reality.

The point is that existence—that is, an actual entity—is always an individual. The next question to pursue is what in the world the "to be" is like, if we take leave of *ri* (the view of reason according to which existence is considered in its connection with universality), by carrying *ji* (the viewpoint of factuality, as it used to be called in the East) to its logical consequence. What then clearly indicates existence in its consummated form is "I" or the self. It is ordinarily described in terms of subjectivity. When referring above to the form of logic, I showed that the relationship between subject and predicate is designated by means of such signs as S and P. In this case, S is regarded as the subject, which has some connection with the subjectivity under consideration. This standpoint of individuality is clearly revealed in the existence of a human being, whose essential feature lies in its irreplaceability.

Appealing to Christianity, Kierkegaard insists that the standpoint of individuality is established when a human being stands before, or in the face of, the Absolute, and he calls this "the absolute relationship to the Absolute." This is because a human being does not always, or necessarily, bear an absolute relation to the Absolute. For instance, God sometimes turns out to be intermingled with social customs and, if so, it happens that we come to believe in God as transformed into these social customs within our social existence. In this case, we always take leave of the standpoint of our being alone, as individuals— that is, of the standpoint from which we are said to return to our authentic selves. Therefore, he emphasizes that the relationship to the Absolute is not a relative one, but absolute; it is a relation worthy of the Absolute. This means that the absolute relation obtains only when we stand on the position of our being alone as individuals. Conversely, this means that it is only in the relationship to the Absolute that we can be said to stand alone.

Thus, it is through Kierkegaard that the use of such words as "existence" and "subjectivity," which had been used in their ordinary sense, came to be burdened with a heavy significance. The credit ascribed to him was not that he added to them an entirely new significance but that he brought out a significance that had been implied from the outset, but was hindered from being brought out fully. I am sure that his criticism of his age occasioned him to perform this task. In this criticism is involved a criticism of both sides. On the front side, he put into practice the criticism of his age, while on the back side, he subjected Christianity itself to severe criticism, such that the predicament of his age was attributed to Christianity. Therefore, we can say that his criticism of his age was the criticism that he had leveled against the predominant Christianity of his times, as seen from the vantage point of his own age. For this reason, his attempt to bring out a new significance in words that had been used since ancient times in order to revitalize them was united with a criticism of his age and society. And with his critique in view, he set forth his reflections upon Christianity, about what Christianity should do or, conversely, what it had failed to do.

The Confucianist Dictum of "Heaven Knows"

On the basis of Kierkegaard's argument as outlined above, Martin Buber raised the question of the relationship between subject and subject, which he called the "I and thou" relation. He proposed that the I-thou was a mutual relationship between two subjects. What is prerequisite in order for this relationship to be established is a standpoint of individuality carried to its logical consequence and a standpoint of not mere individuality, but its absolute negation, that is, as no-selfhood. Subjectivity consists in the fact that the self is, or becomes, a self itself. But another aspect of no-selfhood is involved here. Even as regards the I-thou relationship, we cannot overlook the fact that "thou" comes to relate itself with "I" as a subjectivity of the same sort, or that in the structure of its being there is involved a connection with the other. This can be described in terms of "togetherness" or fellowship. This way of being is an opened-up standpoint. By contrast, individuality is a hidden standpoint that is shut up within itself, where something remains that can by no means be disclosed.

To speak of the same thing in another way, individuality, while possessing something closed, has simultaneously a disclosed side. While being closed within itself, it manifests itself in the form of plurality, just because it exists together with the other through interconnecting with each other in the same actual world. For this reason, absolute singularity is at one with absolute plurality—that is, the absolute one is the same as the absolute two. Here the term "absolute" is used in the sense of "authentic." I think that this is a problem that is dealt with in Buddhism in terms of the "nonduality of oneself and the other." In my view, the mutual relationships of human beings are given due consideration in this way.

Reference was made above to Kierkegaard and Buber as philosophers who had brought this human relationship to a clear-cut delineation, and I am sure that both of them have a religious dimension at the background of their thinking. In the case of Kierkegaard, Christianity, and in that of Buber, Hasidism in the Jewish tradition, are taken as the background.

Such matters have been thought about since ancient times in various ways. As I remarked before, the issue of conscience also somehow comes into being in connection with these considerations. Fundamentally speaking, conscience is intimately connected with the fact that human beings are themselves individuals. It involves something the knowledge of which can be acquired only by oneself, while others cannot share in it. The dictum that conscience does not permit, or that conscience reproaches us, concerns knowledge that is accessible only to oneself, whereas others are completely excluded from it. Ordinarily, conscience is thought to be at the basis of ethics or morality. It is true that in conscience knowledge is only accessible to oneself. But in ancient times, people used to say, in addition, that heaven knows. This phrase quoted is from the proverb "Heaven knows, the earth knows, I know, and others know."

In conscience something is involved of which one feels ashamed, and one feels unsettled and uneasy about it. And this something is that knowledge that is accessible only to oneself, while others are completely excluded from it. But at the same time, we can say that at the place where this "something" is carried to its extreme, the dictum that "Heaven knows" obtains. Knowledge available only to oneself involves an aspect hidden to others. However, I think the dictum "Heaven knows" shows that this hidden aspect comes to be established at the very place where it is opened up. Even though it is concealed to others, this concealment makes its appearance and thus manifests itself at that place which is opened up absolutely, such as in heaven. This place is found somewhere in human existence. And in my opinion, it is what is ordinarily called conscience.

In order to describe this further, we need not necessarily refer to the phrase "Heaven knows." For instance, let us consider the artisan spirit, a rare phenomenon nowadays indeed. Imagine an artist who tries to engage with his works to the extent that they completely satisfy him, even though it results in suffering to his pocketbook. But, it seems to be the current mode of society for workers not to do hard work; they jerry-build, even when under contract.

The case is quite different with the artisan spirit. In this case, a worker continues to engage himself in his work until it completely satisfies him, even though other people tell him to be finished with it. Here the worker is unified with the house that he is engaged in constructing. The affirmation on the part of the worker and that on the part of the house he built come to be established simultaneously. Since the worker and the house become one, he dares to ask other people to look at the house he built, because their looking at it eventually terminates in their looking at him. Conscience is involved here. This argument need not be restricted to workers only. The same can be said of other persons, such as housewives. Since they have work to do, we can say of them that they are brought to self-expression through their own work.

However halfheartedly we may engage in doing our work, there is the possibility of our achievement being highly valued by society. But we cannot be content with that sort of work, nor can we regard it as beneficial merely to ourselves. In connection with this, existence or individuality is spoken of, and it is nothing but conscience, to use old-fashioned terminology. And here a voice arises out of oneself, saying "Is that all right with you?" Moreover, it is not until a voice of reproach, coming from the bottom of one's existence, ceases to be heard that we can say that the matter turns out all right in the end. Socrates calls such reproach his *daemon*, and said that everything can be said to go well only when the *daemon* is silent. This is why he admonishes us to stick to the dictum "Know thyself." To "know thyself" indicates that we should become ourselves. In this case, since "knowledge" is unified with "being," we can say that "being" turns out to be oneself. Even in the East, this has also been taken into consideration since ancient times. But I think it possible to assert that recently, such a fundamental fact has come to be obscured. For this reason, we can say that what constitutes the basic nucleus in workers, housewives, and even in us has been lost sight of.

But there is a place where these two things—that one is oneself and that one bears a relation to others—are truly established. For a carpenter, there is a possibility of bringing into realization the relation that he bears to his employer through the activities of building a house. This possibility is today prevented from being brought into effect because of involvement in financial interests, or by complaints about hard work. In spite of this, however, he may still manage to be recognized as a carpenter by society. But if this is the case, we must say that something in him remains unaccomplished by virtue of which he fails to become an individual in the genuine sense. This is why conscience is summoned. And when it comes to one's conscience, it is always connected with something religious. A worker with conscience does not deliberately refer to the dictum "Heaven knows." But I have the impression that he has an approach toward, or a preparedness for, the religious about which he is ready to let us know, if and when asked. I am convinced that the mutual trust between human beings is rendered impossible, unless we go this far.

The Relationship between One Human Subjectivity and Another

As a consequence of the loss of mutual trust, it seems to me that a way of looking at things has come to the fore that differs from what I have mentioned thus far, including a way through which a human being looks at other human beings. We are able to describe this as science. It is impossible to deal with it briefly, because many problems involved in it will surface. But to use simplified terms, I think it is possible to tackle these issues with the help of the concepts of "substance" and "function," which are usually employed in a contrary fashion. I want to deal with what the term "function" stands for in connection with science.

I have dealt with the individual as well as the universal—or rather, the *eidos* (form). The term "form" designates the law controlling beings—for instance, a universal law in contradistinction to all the things falling under it. I will try to use this term as something universal, that is, as that which brings into synthesis various individuals. Things are multitudinous, and are almost innumerable. But, there are threads that tie multitudinous things together—for instance, such labels as "a pine tree" or "a desk." And it is with these terms in mind that we ordinarily look at things. Our experience comes into being at this level. We cannot live with a world of pure multiplicity alone. Therefore, there must be threads of connection, as well as unifying points. Since our judgment comes into effect in connection with the sense of sight, intellect is already at work when we look at individual things.

Let us consider a hen. If asked what it is, we answer that it is a hen. And asked further what kind of species it belongs to, we answer that it is a bird, and if we extend our argument a step further, that it belongs to the category of living things. This is one way of dealing with it. But there is another way according to which we deal with it as a chicken. In the latter case, we have in mind a way of thinking according to which we look at it as an animal protein, that is, as something to be eaten, instead of as a concrete individual hen. I am sure that this is clearer in the case of a steer. In English, we refer to this animal as a bull or cow. But when reference is made to it as food, we use the word "beef." In Japanese, we do not say that "we eat a steer," but that "we eat beef." The reason for it lies, after all, in the fact that there is a difference in meaning between the word "steer," and the word "beef." When it comes to beef, the meaning of a living being is erased. When we speak of a steer or a hen, we cannot completely wipe away the feeling aroused by the above-mentioned I-thou relationship. In the case of human beings, this relationship stands out in most conspicuous relief, as I said before. But the I-thou relationship obtains between one thing and another, irrespective of whether it is a steer, a bird, a stone, or even a tree. When we love a stone or a tree, we are in the I-thou relationship with it. With beef or flesh, however, we no longer stand in the I-thou relationship, but treat it as animal-protein. This is why Buber accounts for this relationship by means of the I-it relation, instead of the I-thou. Here the term "it" refers to the third person, recognized as an object instead of a subject. The same can be said of the relation to human beings. To deal with them as tools that are useful or beneficial to us is to recognize them not as genuine subjects, but as objects. By virtue of the fact that this is a closed standpoint—that is, a self-centered standpoint devoid of a place called no-selfhood that is susceptible to allowing others to live as others—there is no possibility of others being recognized as subjects instead of as objects. They simply turn out to be objects. The same can be said of a bird or a steer when it is simply treated as flesh.

If we push our argument about individuals further and further, then it turns out that what we envision is a living person, or a hen. Thus, what finally surfaces is a way of looking at things as substances. But if we proceed to look at a hen in the form of protein, it is then recognized as something material, instead of as a living hen. To deal with it as something pertaining to protein is to look at it in terms of function. Since protein is susceptible to being divided into various elements, then if we carry on our analysis further and further, this results in looking at it as a compound of physiochemical elements. In this way, distinction must be made between these two ways of looking at things.

When we start from the individual, and then enlarge our view to consider this individual as a hen, on the one hand, and when we argue that this hen provides us with flesh, on the other hand, we are exemplifying the two approaches used whenever we think about things. So far as the concept of flesh is concerned, it is applied not only to a hen or an ox, but also even to a human being. Since in its application, its concept is not restricted to something specific, it is said to be the larger universal itself inclusive of other universals.

Therefore, I think that what is at stake here are the individual, the particular, and the universal. The particular is a kind of universal. But this is so insofar as it is a universal that is directly connected with individuals, and is thus immanent in them. When attention is paid to flesh, in the midst of considering particulars such as hens and steers, it is said that reference is made to the universal, which is one degree greater than the universals grasped in the form of particulars. If we proceed in our argument from hens, we are focused on individuals. But if our attention is paid to flesh in the wider sense, then the individual passes out of our sight.

The Standpoint of the Natural Sciences and Human Alienation

It can be said that science has a position that is, in a sense, aloof from human beings, for it submits things to objective reflection by taking on a perspective transcendent to human feelings and desires, and tries to know the laws that preside over things. However, it has a tendency to dissolve the being of individual things. I think that such a way of looking at things is already manifest in the way in which natural scientists look at nature, and that its most conspicuous manifestation is found in the so-called modern technique represented by machines, which have arisen through the application of scientific knowledge. I am sure that the cause of environmental pollution originates herein. Pollution has to do with the relation between human beings and their environment. But the most basic problem here is that human beings busy themselves with techniques so much that they forget the most important fact that they live in the midst of the environment. In this case, the human body itself seems not to be given due consideration, for we are connected to the environment through our bodies. And it goes without saying that we cannot maintain our lives without air, water, and so forth. This can be said not only of human beings but of animals and plants as well. Air circulates in such a way that the air I breathe is in turn breathed by someone else, and the air a plant breathes is in turn breathed by me. And water also goes around the sky, falls to the earth, and then is available to animals and plants living on the earth. We can say that water and air are essential means of our life. The human body is, from the outset, unified with the world of nature in such a way that it is impossible to separate the two. It is a part of what comprises the natural world.

In contrast, the natural scientific standpoint has a tendency to deal with the human body in a physiochemical manner, and tries to investigate it as mere matter, and its physiological functions as mere phenomena of matter from a perspective quite aloof from that of actual human beings. As for medical science, its basic standpoint seems to consist in treating a disease as a natural phenomenon, and it makes no distinction between a healthy state and an ill one, insofar as both of them are taken to be one and the same natural phenomenon. I admit that a distinction is generally made between medical science and medical technique. The basic standpoint of the latter is humanistic, because its major business lies in rescuing human beings from their pain. But fundamentally speaking, medical science and medical technique cannot be separated from one another. Scientific research is carried on for the sake of rescuing human beings, but it is generally held that the most basic way to cure diseases and to maintain a healthy state lies in acquiring knowledge as to how to deal with problems of the human body as a natural phenomenon quite apart from human beings and without consideration of their diseases. These two sides seem to be contradictory. In other words, the aspect of "I-thou" and that of objectively looking at things as "I-it" combine to give birth to scientific medical investigation. This seems to be the reason why medical techniques have an aspect that is benevolent. It bears some connection with the religious.

Even from a religious standpoint, there is an aspect of compassion, like the act of benevolence, and another aspect that is a disinterested observing, an attitude that in Buddhism is described as "knowing things as they really are." These seemingly contradictory attitudes were immanent in Buddhism from the outset. Let us take suffering as an example. While in the midst of pain, we at the same time try to observe our suffering state as it really is, in the same manner in which a medical doctor observes diseases as natural phenomena. Otherwise, it would be impossible for us to have a clear grasp of the Buddhist truth of suffering. In order to have this sense of suffering, it is no good not to have had the experience of suffering, nor to involve oneself in pain that results in one's writhing in desperate agony. For the Pure Land Sect of Buddhism, knowledge that lies in the background is gradually transformed into the Buddha's knowledge and Buddha's light, which are combined with Buddha's compassion. In my view, a similar juxtaposition is also to be found at the background of medical science.

With respect to scientific techniques or mechanical techniques, it must be remarked that the fact that human beings cannot live without air or water was put aside, until we began to suffer from difficulties such as air pollution and water pollution. This clearly indicates that, fundamentally speaking, a scientific standpoint does not pay heed to air and water except as resources to be utilized. And it has come to pass that such a scientific standpoint has been transformed, just as it is, into technologies that give rise to mechanical techniques.

What was said above involves the natural sciences directly. But almost the same can be said of the social sciences, which are also concerned with environmental pollution. For these sciences tend to attach importance only to the structure of organization as such with no thought of living human beings. What is thought of as something problematic in communist-oriented societies, as well as in capitalist-oriented ones, is, after all, the management organization. But the basic problem threatening on a grand scale is not so much management organization, but rather the tendency to look at human beings with the aim of organizing all of them without exception. It is often remarked that attempts have been made to make human beings into the cogs of a gigantic structure or machine. From what has been said above, the conclusion can be drawn that through science, no matter whether natural or social, priority is given to looking at things functionally instead of substantially. In the case of the natural sciences, matters are dealt with by substituting mere forces or energy. That is to say, science reduces them to the motion of energy. We can describe this procedure by using the term "function" in the broad sense. The term "function" is also used in mathematics. So if we try to give expression to this procedure in a mathematical fashion, the terminology of functional relation is readily accessible. The essential features of this procedure lie in reducing matters to quantitatively calculable relations. What plays a main role here is the attempt to give expression to material things in terms of energy or forces.

Let us turn our attention to relationships within human societies. Human societies tend to be organized functionally, and come to be thought of as machines with a single purpose. Take a modern company as an example. Before the modern age, there was the possibility of a human being feeling at home and comfortable after returning to his or her place of residence. But since then, we have suffered from a kind of homelessness, in which atomic individuals insist on their own rights and are separated from each other without ever entering into genuine human relations. Furthermore, we can say that the same tendency predominates in the relations between parents and children, as well as between husband and wife.

The Buddhist Concept of "Interdependent Origination"

The main theme of our inquiry has been to submit the human body to a reconsideration. We can say that human beings and the world of nature are connected as one, due to the fact that we cannot live without air and water. The world of nature is a field in which human beings are rendered capable of existing. And the world, as the field of human existence, and human beings who exist in it are united. This means that human beings are incorporated into nature so completely that they constitute only a part of the world of nature. Water, for instance, circulates around the world of nature, and human beings are involved in this circulation. The same is true not only of human beings, but also of animals and plants. All of them are alive by virtue of this fact. They are all parts of nature. It is impossible to separate them from the world of nature. But, a human body possesses another aspect as well: it is also a human being. This issue I have already dealt with in previous lectures.

Incidentally, such things as water and air belong to the nonliving, inorganic world. And it is said that these things are essential in maintaining our lives. Above, I remarked that a human body is a human being. However, between such things as water and air, on the one hand, and the human body, on the other, we have one more item to consider, for there is a stage in which we think of our living in a clearer way. Since early times, we have attempted to conceive of nature by regarding it as a living organic whole, instead of paying attention only to air and water. This must be explained

Exactly what is involved here? We can say that all things come to be, and perish, and thus are set in a "becoming and flow." It is not that all things merely "are," but that they become; they undergo transformation and thus are set in "motion and flow." Judging from this, we can say that for a thing to "be" means that it nevertheless springs out of the world of nature, undergoes transformations, and finally returns to it again. In this case, nature is regarded as a living whole. The whole universe is here conceived of as a world of becoming and change, and as the field in which the motion and flow of all things that come to arise and disappear occur. Lying in the background is the view that all things, including human beings, emerge from and enter into the world. And from this viewpoint, the world as a whole is regarded as alive. I am convinced that this way of thinking is the same as that by means of which we conceive of the human body or mind.

Buddhism has the idea of "interdependent origination," according to which all things are conceived of as being related to one another through causality in such a way that one thing causes another to emerge. For instance, the reason why I exist lies in my having parents, who were in turn dependent upon their parents, and so forth. And to speak of the matter differently, a child becomes a parent, who in turn gives birth to a child, and so forth. This simplified example shows that the cause-effect relation holds sway over beings as such. We can say that in addition to this, however, there is behind the phenomena of being another aspect, in accordance with which it can certainly be said that I come out of my parents, but at the same time this is also not the case. For we did not come out of our parents insofar as the basis of our being is concerned. For instance, keeping an eye on the fact that "I am," I cannot say even that my parents could possibly have produced this fact, as it really is. Hence, God or Buddha must come on the scene. Perhaps this is the origin of the idea that a child is God's gift. In this sense, we can say that parents, too, have this same origin, instead of being born from their parents alone. With regard to our own children, it follows that it is not that we gave birth to them, despite the fact that we did so, biologically speaking. Judging from the place where "beings" come into question, we can certainly say that they come from their parents. Here the relation of cause and effect obtains. But if the question is raised about the basis of beings as such—that is, about Being—then something like the arising of Being from Nothingness must be pursued. So far as the arising and perishing of beings is concerned, we cannot dispose of this issue by simply referring to a phrase such as "from their parents," but instead we must think of this phenomenon as arising from a deeper origin, which it may not be beside the mark to describe as the center of the world. Here there is neither beginning nor end. What is called becoming cannot be comprehended apart from the world. It must be said that the world brings forth its changes under the guise of such events. Thus, we are inevitably led to think that the world is a disclosure that comes forward as a question to be asked. My position is simply to point out that the self comes to be established without exception in and through such a disclosure.

As a consequence, even though I have made mention of the causal relation, we cannot dispose of it simply by referring to the succession of life from parents to child. Another aspect of the matter is also involved, for both parents and child can be said to arise from the same origin. With this in mind, we can say that the causal relation now comes to be recognized in a cubic fashion. This is what I mean by saying that nature is alive and that it is that through which something novel incessantly arises. Readers are advised to recollect the illustration of "water and waves." What is at stake is the direction in which "I" who was born from my parents and "I" who am not born from them are now thought of as united into one.

I think that the problem of life, as well as that of "interdependent origination" must be considered in connection with the world of creatures.

The Double Characteristic of the Human Body

Now let us leave the problem of life for a while and pay attention to the "I" in the above-mentioned phrase "I-thou." This "I" is an acting agent with self-conscious knowledge in view. Here is a full-fledged practical standpoint in contradistinction to "becoming and flow." By taking advantage of the knowledge that includes within itself even knowledge about nature (that is, knowledge of the laws of nature), subjectivity tries to establish its own world (that is, the sociohistorical world). This world is no longer the world of nature, but the world that human beings have constructed with clear-cut consciousness out of the world of nature. Therefore it is called history, culture, or human society. I think that this brings into focus various problems, including those concerned with the sciences. In my opinion, two poles are entangled within the human body. One of them is that the human body is an element constituting the world of nature; the other is that it is the "I" that sets in motion the world of nature by standing aloof from it, and by manipulating knowledge and techniques. And the human body lives, somehow, in between these two poles.

I am convinced that faith is of great importance, particularly when inquiring into religious concerns. Because of this, we have not yet given a full-fledged consideration of the meaning that the human body bears to the religious. What I mean is that "the human body" is not a material object, but the "I" in the sense that this human body is "I." When I beat another person, it is not that two physical bodies have clashed with each other, but that the I-thou is involved here, through which the human body of "I" beats that of "thou." There are many cases in which the I-thou relation cannot be expressed except through the human body.

The Human Body is Connected with the Land of One's Own Country

There are many further questions to be asked about the human body. Let me enumerate the essential points here. Keeping an eye on the way in which the human body is tied to water and soil, we can say that the concept of the land and of one's country surfaces as being of great significance. Tetsurō Watsuji once published a book whose title is *Climate and Culture*. He investigated the characteristics of those born in the climate of Japan. If a Japanese has had the opportunity to live in a foreign country for a while, he would have frequently desired to eat miso soup or *tsukemono*, a kind of pickle. This indicates that the connection that our human body bears to the land continues to come to the fore. If we only eat the food that is prevalent in foreign countries most of the time, then this induces us to want to eat rice and miso soup. This bears witness to the fact that the human body cannot be cut off from the water and the soil, and is thus united with the land of his or her country. Nature also comes to be dealt with in this same way.

I have had this same experience. When I ate miso soup after a long absence, while living in a foreign country, I came to realize how good miso soup tasted. It is not enough merely to say that it tasted good. I felt at that time that it fundamentally tasted good. At that very moment I was compelled to become conscious of the fact that I was a Japanese. This indicates, after all, that food reaches to the root of my existence, such that the mere remark that it tasted very good was not enough. What continually surfaces here is the question of our connection with the land and the country. I am sure that it is true not only of food, but also of the arts of human culture, and even of religion, as somehow based on the land of the country. Otherwise, something authentic would be prevented from coming forth. Things that belong to no country cannot be evaluated as authentic. On the contrary, only those things that have genuinely taken root in their own country are eligible to be considered to have a universality. At first sight, this statement seems to be contradictory. But this is not so.

But, there is something else to be noticed here. Scientific knowledge should also be given due consideration. Today's intelligentsia tend to think of things in a scientific or a logical fashion in one way or another. But the most basic issue is that, in addition to knowledge acquired through intellect, there is knowledge that is acquired through the human body. Here the human body is once more the issue. To acquire knowledge to the extent that it becomes a real appropriation means that it has been simplified from its complex connections of concepts, so that we can understand it without struggling to explain it. We come to have such a clear understanding of this that, if asked to explain it, we would be at a loss as to what to say, and in the final analysis, there seems to be no alternative but to come to understand it by ourselves. Knowledge acquired in this way has such significance that it is always alive and at work. I am convinced that religious knowledge is of this sort. It is not knowledge to be learned through the head. Even the highly evaluated Buddhist knowledge, if it is learned in this way, is not the knowledge that Buddhism has in mind, but is regarded as ordinary learning. To acquire genuine knowledge, or to realize enlightenment and Buddhist truth, means to acquire knowledge in such a way that it becomes a real appropriation.

By contrast, scientific knowledge is not smoothly or easily appropriated through the human body. Perhaps it was different with geniuses such as Newton and Einstein. But the scientific knowledge we learn at school cannot be acquired as a bodily appropriation. It is only when it is transformed into techniques that we can be said to have acquired it as a bodily appropriation. In this case, however, we must say that we have truly appropriated it under the guise of techniques through machines, rather than through our human bodies. In some

ways we can say that computers or robots are constructed by transforming the human body into these machines. But I am also sure that
we cannot thereby acquire knowledge in such a way that it really
becomes our bodily appropriation. Therefore, such knowledge acquisition is not susceptible to leading us toward religious enlightenment.
It is knowledge that will make us neither foolish, nor enlightened. As
for being foolish, there are some elements that we are able to comprehend. In a situation in which we genuinely understand something,
there is one respect in which we do return to being a fool—namely by
forsaking scientific knowledge completely. It has been remarked that
knowledge is genuinely established only when the scholar's knowledge has been completely abandoned. That knowledge which authentically comes to be established by having abandoned the scholar's
knowledge completely is referred to as spiritual awakening. This is in
accordance with the dictum that one comes to understand Buddha-
nature by becoming oneself a fool who is incapable of understanding
even one sentence. There is a difference of expression between Zen
Buddhism and Shin Buddhism on this point. But both of them share
something in common in asserting that for us to learn, we must be
fools, and that foolishness is somehow affiliated with true knowledge.
Be this as it may, I am convinced that knowledge of this sort cannot
arise in the sciences.

Because of its association with the land of the country, the human
body develops a variety of characteristics that can be described through
such phrases as "to acquire knowledge in such a way that it becomes
a real bodily appropriation," "to come home to one's body," or "to
take a bodily interest in something." The phrase "to take a bodily
interest in something" means to absorb oneself wholeheartedly in it.
I think that taking a bodily interest in things provides us with a clue
as to how to think about the world of religion.

Above, I referred to the distinction between the world of nature
and that of history. My point was to render it possible for human
beings to come back to nature once again through their various activities. Human activity arises out of nature understood in the broadest
sense, and even though human beings have produced the various
sciences and technology as a means of struggling against nature, their
ability to do these things was granted by nature, rather than arising
from their own abilities alone. Human beings are born with a human
body, and they are also gifted with this ability. And this ability is
given a further impetus to produce culture. But the basic fact is that
this ability is a granted one. This indicates that behind the domain in
which the human volition or the self of the "I-thou" is established,

there lurks another, more basic nature—that is, a world that is thought
of as being at the base of, and as inclusive of, the subjective. If we are
allowed to call this world the land of the country, the land appears
here as the basis on which to conceive of the relation between the
issue of the religious land and the human body. It is generally held in
Shin Buddhism that the Pure Land is cut off from this impure one.
However, I hold the view that these two lands are somehow tied up
with each other. In our traditional way of thinking, we have the word
jinen. We Japanese have used it to refer to nature, even though *jinen*
is meant to refer to the unification of two meanings—namely, natural-
ness and spontaneity. I think that the Buddhist word *jinen,* in the
phrase "the Pure Land of *jinen,*" alludes to that which goes beyond the
historical activities of human beings, and yet is inclusive of them.

I think we can now advance a little in dealing with the problem of
how the world of human history and the world of nature are related.
Behind our attempt to regard the actual world as the world of history,
there is the world conceived of in terms of "interdependent origination"
and the world referred to in physics. By taking on these worlds as my
standpoint, I would like to embark upon a consideration about the
world of human beings and the world of religion, both of which stand
out in clear-cut relief as matters needing to be explored further.

History in Buddhism

History is something with which it is quite difficult to cope. But
if asked whether or not there is a possible way to tackle it, I will
answer in the affirmative. I am sorry to be so abrupt, but I would like
to refer here to the Buddhist phrase "to be equal to the Tathāgata," or
"to be equal to the bodhisattva called Miroku." The Buddha called
Miroku is a history-oriented bodhisattva who is coming to this world
in the future. Then what does the phrase "to be equal to Miroku"
mean? Miroku seems not to have become a Buddha yet, and at the
same time, to have become a Buddha already. So far as Amida Buddha
is concerned, I get the impression that he is already an accomplished
Buddha who constitutes both the beginning and the basis of all other
things. What impresses and attracts me is that Miroku is spoken of
here as going ahead of us. The phrase "to be equal to Miroku" has to
do with *shōjōjū*—that is, the stage of the truly settled at which a be-
liever is assured of becoming Buddha, a stage to be attained in the
future. If this stage or faith arises at a place where the impure land
and the Pure Land intersect, and where the light from the two sides

shines on each other, then this must be the place where "to be equal to Miroku" obtains. When Miroku is spoken of, we are sometimes inclined to think that we are waiting for the future with our hands folded. But this is not true. Since it is said that we are able to become equal to Miroku in our looking to the future, I think that a great possibility is opened up, encouraging us to create the future by devoting much of our time to Buddhist activities.

I have heard that faith in Miroku has played an important role in the history of Buddhism, and there are certainly many sūtras concerning Miroku. I think it is of significance that Shinran, while having immersed himself in the knowledge of Miroku, referred to the phrase "to be equal to Miroku."

However this may be, let me dwell on history a little longer. I mentioned earlier the relation between tradition and the future. But the point is that the past is opened up through the future, and the future is opened up through the past. And the present, that arises as the point in which these two directions intersect allows us to submit once more to reconsideration not only the problem of human beings but also that of the Pure Land. These problems involve sociohistorical issues, characterized in terms of the sacred-secular two-truths doctrine. I also feel that it is necessary for us to think about the Pure Land as the basis of human existence. When it comes to nirvāna and when it comes to the Pure Land of *jinen*, it seems necessary for us to reconsider them in the context of the whole structure of Buddhism, in which nirvāna and the Pure Land of *jinen* are conceived of in close connection with the testimony that we bear to great nirvāna in this world. After that, we must think about these matters in connection with current issues to be dealt with in the present world. I think it important for the younger generation to step forward in this way without being afraid of making a few mistakes.

Part Three

———

On Conscience

5

In Support of Human Relations

Confucianism's Influence on the Formation of Ethics in Japan

Last year, I had the opportunity to lecture here. At that time I referred to conscience as that which is said to reproach us. I would like to continue to talk about this topic this year.

Truthfully, I have never pondered the issue of conscience in detail. But since it is an important issue with relevance to various matters, and since I have occasionally reflected upon it, it is my pleasure now to share my thinking about it. To begin with, I would like to repeat in brief outline what I mentioned last year, because I myself do not remember it in detail.

The term "conscience" is ordinarily used in the sense that conscience reproaches, as I have already said. In this sense, it is tied up with morality or ethics. When we have the issues of ethics in view, conscience stands out in sharp relief as a matter of great concern. The Japanese word *ryōshin*, which we use at present, is perhaps meant to refer to the word as used in the Western world. For conscience is there discussed in intimate connection with the issues of ethics. *Ryōshin* is equivalent to the word "conscience," which seems to have been translated into Japanese as *ryōshin* ever since the Meiji era. But there is no clear evidence for this. It is in connection with ethics that the word *ryōshin* is generally used among Japanese people. This way of using it is the same as in the Western world. We modern Japanese deal with it as an ethics-oriented word. The case is the same in the West. This does not mean, however, that there has not been in Japan, since ancient times, a use of the word *ryōshin* written by means of kanji.

It was through Confucianism, and particularly through the school of Chu Hsi, which had its start in the T'ang and Sung periods, that the term *ryōshin* came to bear an important meaning. I do not think it necessary to speak of this topic in detail here. However, it was through

111

this school that Confucianism began to develop a tinge of highly organized philosophical thought. When reference is made to this newly
developing Confucianism, we ordinarily have in mind the school of
Wang, which had its debut through Wang Yang-ming, after the Sung
period. But concerning this history, we ordinarily give precedence to
the school of Chu Hsi over the school of Yōmeigaku. The famous
collection of the sayings of Wang Yang-ming entitled *Denshūroku* is
readily available, and many people are familiar with it. This book
exercised great influence. In this book, the term *ryōshin* is frequently
used, together with the term *ryōchi* (good knowledge) or *ryōnō* (good
capacity). That the term *shin* (mind) in *ryōshin* came to bear an important significance indicates that the school of Chu Hsi, and Wang Yang-
ming in particular, had been greatly influenced by Buddhism. It is
generally held that Zen Buddhism exerted the most conspicuous influence upon Wang Yang-ming. The essential feature of Buddhism is to
keep aloof from worldly affairs. In my view, the unworldliness peculiar to Buddhism results from the fact that it refused to engage itself
in mundane affairs such as politics and economics.

I am convinced that Buddhism somehow felt compelled to think
that mundane affairs fall short of advancing a human being's way of
life to its logical consequence. It is because Buddhism keeps itself from
the affairs of this world that the school of Chu Hsi is quite critical of
Buddhism. The core of this criticism is an attack on Buddhism's aloofness from this world. What path did the newly developed standpoint
of Confucianism try to follow? On the one hand, it too stood aloof from
worldly affairs. But on the other hand, it tried to attach great importance to the mundane life, or, to use the term characteristic of Buddhism, to the life of the layman, especially to society, politics, ethics, or,
to use a current term, moral issues. I think that in this manner it tried
to pave the way toward distinguishing itself from Buddhism.

In the beginning, this new version of Confucianism leveled quite
severe criticism against Buddhism. When we take these criticisms, we
may well gain the impression that it was raised not so much by having genuinely understood what Buddhism really meant but rather by
viewing things from a Confucian standpoint without being sufficiently
immersed in Buddhism. Be this as it may, the fact is that the school of
Chu Hsi took quite a critical attitude toward Buddhism. At the same
time, those who were scholars affiliated with Chu Hsi—that is, repre-
sentatives of the newly fashioned Confucianism—had, without exception, an intimate relation with Zen Buddhism. In books written by
these scholars, there often appears terminology affiliated with Zen
Buddhism. Nonetheless, Chu Hsi's school, as well as Wang Yang-

ming's is very critical of Buddhism with respect to the latter's aloofness from the world. It is because of this that I hold the view that *ryōshin* was first brought into relief by Wang Yang-ming.

The Issue of the Mind

The term *ryōshin* was not only used to refer to ethics, as is now the case with what we use as a translation of the term "conscience" prevalent in the West, but also to refer to something in a far broader sense. The mind itself is referred to whenever the term *ryōshin* (whose literal Japanese meaning is "good mind") is spoken of. The mind is accounted for not only through recourse to psychology, as what happens to the mind of a human being, but also as that which is affiliated with and permeated by all of the things in the world, including human beings. When we think of the term *ryōshin* in this broad sense, we can say, in the final analysis, that it is here used in such a grand-scale way and with such a widespread background that it leads us to find its extension to and affiliation with Buddha-nature, to use Buddhist terminology once again.

For instance, when mention is made of "Buddha-mind," it is not only that this mind is regarded as something associated, in the psychological sense, with the mind of each person. Rather (to push the argument to its extreme), it is also conceived of as being in the midst of the world in which grasses grow, flowers come into bloom, birds sing, and there are mountains and rivers. To advance our argument a step further, when Buddha-mind is spoken of, it is taken into account as a field that is inclusive of all the things in the world. Such a perspective is inherent in Buddhism.

Keeping an eye on this aspect, it seems to me that the Buddhist sects that hold to the doctrine of salvation through works have conceived of the issue of mind from such a broad background. The most outstanding example of this is Zen Buddhism. This is why it was and is still called the Buddha-mind sect. When Buddha-mind is conceived of from the standpoint of Zen Buddhism, it is oftentimes remarked that "a willow is green and a flower is crimson." In and through the very fact that a willow is green and a flower is crimson, the mind is glimpsed in Zen Buddhism, and so it is called the Buddha-mind sect. In addition to this, the Buddha-mind is also meant to indicate the center or ground of the mind of each human being. This is why Zen Buddhism speaks of the ground of mind.

If we go so far as to the ground of a human being's mind, the world in which flowers come into bloom and a willow is swayed by the wind cannot be separated from the ground of a human being's mind. Fundamentally speaking, they are tied up with each other. Buddha-mind is conceived of as manifesting itself at the most basic place where they are tied together. On the one hand, this Buddhist view has a philosophical implication. But on the other, it admonishes us to return to Buddha-mind, and to find there the authentic path of a human being. What I want to say here is that ethics or morality is here established on this authentic path.

Mention is made here of *rinri* (ethics). This Japanese term seems to be difficult to understand, but *rin* refers to fellowship—that is, human relations, which it is appropriate for us to describe in terms of the relationship between one human being and another. A human being is conceived of not as alone, but as in relationship with others. As a result, human relationships bear a very important significance to us as human beings. This is what the term *rin* means.

Then what does the term *ri* mean? I think that it is concerned with what a human relation should be like, or how a sacred human relationship comes to be established, if I may be allowed to use the term "sacred." *Ri* has something to do with the sacred form, reason, or thread of connection that renders a human relation capable of being genuine. At the same time, *ri* renders it necessary for us to have this sacred relation mutually in order to become genuine human beings and teaches us what attitudes we should take toward others, or what deeds we should perform insofar as we are in this sacred relationship with another. *Rinri* is concerned with the task of indicating what form a genuine human relationship should take, or basically with the problem of encouraging each human being to become what he or she should be.

Thus, we can say that there is some difference between human beings and animals, and that from the outset it is insufficient for a human being to be a mere human being alone. It is here clearly revealed that it is only when a human being becomes genuine that he or she is eligible to be called a human being. Therefore, in order that we may say that he or she is a human being in the genuine sense of the word, it is necessary for each individual to become an authentic human being.

There is yet one more question to be asked. What should we do in order to become an authentic human being? To this we answer that each of us must do our utmost, or take pains to achieve this end. The phrase "take pains" means that we must render ourselves capable of being, becoming, or building up an authentic human being out of ourselves. This is the aspect in which a human being differs from an animal. What happens in the case of an animal? Let us take a dog as our example. We can certainly say that it must become a genuine dog, in order that it may be a dog. But this does not stand out in clear-cut relief. In other words, in the case of an animal or a plant, morality or ethics does not come into question. More fundamentally speaking, a human being is provided with freedom. In addition to freedom, he or she also has knowledge. In these two respects, there is a difference between a human being and an animal.

To sum up, in order to say that a man or woman is a human being, it is necessary for him or her to become an authentic human being. In order that he or she may become an authentic human being, he or she must achieve becoming an authentic human being out of himself or herself, instead of becoming a human being by letting everything go as it likes. We must go so far as to say that we "achieve" becoming a human being by going beyond the realm where we "become" it. That a human being *is* means that he or she should achieve authenticity, or that he or she is in such a way that he or she should be just that. Here, "to be" involves such an implication. This is a characteristic peculiar to a human being that makes us different from other animals.

The Feature Characteristic of Being Human

From this we can draw the conclusion that ethics is a question quite fundamental for a human being. We are accustomed to thinking of ethics as something to be kept at a distance. But the basic problem of ethics lies in the fact that it is unavoidably involved at the basis by means of which a human being exists as a human being. To achieve this status, or to become a human being is not something that is only a problem for each individual. That we become or achieve genuine human beingness means that we proceed to create or to build up out of ourselves a genuine human being through our own capacities and through our daily activities. Here there is involved an implication of "achieving."

That we "achieve" being a human being in the above sense implies, it seems to me, that each of us ought to be so. But we cannot dispose of the matter only by saying this. When it is said that we achieve being a human being, it is not only the case that we ourselves become so, but we also render other persons capable of becoming truly human as well. To advance a step further, we achieve being human so that other persons may also become human beings. In other words, it is not the case that we do not care what other persons become, or that everything goes well if we mind only our own affairs, no matter how much this bothers other persons. To say that every-thing goes well only when we are capable of becoming a human being at the expense of other persons seems to plunge us into a contradic-tion, if the verdict is delivered from the standpoint of achieving genu-ine human status.

If we ourselves try to become genuine human beings while sac-rificing others and leaving them to be tossed about by the winds and waves, I think that this will prevent us from achieving this end. If we want to become genuine human beings, it is necessary for us to relate to other persons in such a way that we render them capable of becom-ing genuine human beings. The more one takes an attitude that shows no concern for other persons, worrying only about oneself, the farther one is from becoming a genuine human being. That we achieve genu-inely being human cannot be separated from the activities through which we entice others, especially those who come into direct contact with us, to become genuine human beings. Here lies the basic way of a human being. I am convinced that if we take leave of this basic way of living, we simply cannot become genuine human beings.

Now let's turn our attention to the relation between one individual and another. Even though it is a leap in the argument to suddenly move from individual human relations to a society, I am sure that at the basis of social and human relations in the broad sense there lurks an insepa-rable connection. I think that the term "ethics" is based upon this.

Ethics is conceived of concretely as something prevalent at various places and in various forms of human relations. Take the family as an illustration. The family is one of the great issues with which ethics is concerned. It goes without saying that a family consists of two rela-tions—that is, a husband and a wife, on the one hand, and parents and children, on the other. It thus arises at the place where the vertical and the horizontal relations are tied up with each other. Recently, reference has frequently been made to the nuclear family, which is constituted only by husband and wife, that is, a male and a female. But if we look only at this aspect of a family, we must say that it falls short of the authentic family. It is a one-sided family. I think that a family without the parent-child relationship falls short of being an authentic family. Within the conjugal relation it is natural that a child is born.

Contraception has become popular among the younger genera-tion. And I get the impression that the birth of a child now hangs in mid air. If we think of a home or a family, we must take marriage seriously, to say the least. There is a tendency among young people to conceive of a marriage as a sort of love affair—that is, as a temporal relation that is obtained on the spot between a man and a woman. If this is the case, the genuine meaning of a family does not emerge. You may conceive of a family as something like a friendly relation or a love affair, but the fact still remains that you have your own parents and have been brought up by them. Therefore, if you want to truly love each other, you must have your own child and foster it. In a marriage, this is the minimum requirement.

If this is so, it comes to pass that a marriage must have a clear-cut and fixed form. And there, a thread of connection comes to the fore as something very important: a filial duty or a mutual love between a husband and a wife. And, after all, there intervenes a sort of morality. Even though it is admitted that many problems arise in connection with this, the established fact is that parents are to be affectionate to their children and children are to be obedient to their parents. Let us now put aside for a while the question of what filial duty is. Be this as it may, we must, at any rate, recognize that here again ethics comes into question.

For instance, the issue of a family has, in reality, something to do with the basis of a human being. We must take for granted the fact that this basic structure is now in process of collapse, particularly in the so-called advanced countries. And the question of whether or not we are able to dispose of the matter only by saying that these phenomena are a kind of corruption must be dealt with in an extremely deliberate fashion. For all that has been called ethical in a traditional sense cannot now be evaluated as necessarily right. Let us take the family relation as our example. There are a variety of problems here— for instance, the relations between parents and children, between a mother-in-law and a daughter-in-law, and between husband and wife. The balance of power within a family varies in accordance with a husband's assertion of his authority, or else a wife holds her head high, as is frequently seen. In this way, we can say that new problems have arisen in family relations as society develops.

One more thing to be raised here is the period in which ethics is taken into consideration. We cannot treat lightly the verdict that traditional ethics is bad because of its being old-fashioned, and that one had better lay aside such an old-fashioned ethics. As I said before, if we stuck to this verdict, we would fall into a contradiction. Young people are inclined to think that the best way for a human being to revitalize humanity is to live freely without restriction, and that to give full scope to humanity consists in taking leave of ethics. But if you think in this way, there are many cases in which you come into conflict with yourself such that you will be deceived by this very thought. I am afraid that, in the way of thinking prevalent among young people today, there are many such situations that led them to cry bitterly in secret.

The fault with the young consists in making a jump from the premise that ethics is of no use because of its being old-fashioned to the conclusion that it is out of date to speak of ethics at all. This does not hold true. Instead, if we push the pursuit of what it means to be a human being to its consequence, we must confront ethics all the time as an issue that is to be newly probed. What is required of us concerning ethics is always to take it seriously as the ought-to-be path for a human being. And it is always necessary for us to have a position from which to critically inquire into the question of where the fault lies with old-fashioned ethics; of what the newly arising human relation consists in, in contradistinction from the old-fashioned; and of where a defect lies within family relations. For these purposes, ethics is indispensable, after all. These are the problems that we must delve into deeply, and which we must ponder clearheadedly. I think it necessary to pursue ethics as far as possible as a critical basis from which to cope with problems arising in the actual world.

The Buddhist Concept of "Skill in Means"

Even though my talk may have deviated a bit from the main theme, my point was to make clear that the family is one of the great issues with which ethics is concerned.

That a family is an important issue is true, it seems to me, not only for Japan but also for other advanced countries, such as Europe and the United States of America. It is usually held that the general public in these countries does not have a crisis consciousness concerning this issue. Let us take up the issue of divorce as a familiar example. In the United States, there are many married couples who have experienced divorce a few times over. We are surprised by this frequency. But then, the real problem is: what happens to a child? It becomes entangled in a very complex destiny. I cannot shake the fear that the place a child occupies in a family has become obscured to a great extent. For instance, the following story is not a rare phenomenon. A married couple I happened to meet consisted of a father who brought three children with him, and whose mothers were different in each case. One of them is a child from his first marriage, the second a child from his second marriage, and the third a child from his present marriage. When asked about it, the third child answered that it is now living with its mother and that, even though its mother is separated from her husband, she is not yet divorced. This confession was so complicated that I could not quite understand it. It is all right for adult people to do such things at their own pleasure, but if we enter into a child's heart, I am unable to erase my anxiety about what its heart becomes, as it grows up. I might be accused of a tradition-oriented way of thinking. In spite of this, I get the impression that the relation between parents and a child, if driven to utter confusion, elicits very grave problems. I have no word to describe this state of affairs except in terms of its being "complicated and inscrutable." I was informed that there would be under enactment a law with which to provisionally solve such issues as the social system. Judging from the fact that the problem is not concerned merely with the social system, but rather with the living relation between human beings, I am afraid that grave and troublesome problems will inevitably arise. Now at issue is the care of mind, which is to some extent overlooked in the United States. I am sure that the same tendency is more and more likely to arise in Japan, as time goes on.

In brief, there is a growing tendency for ethics to lose its weight. The authentic cause of this tendency lies in the fact that Christianity, which has so far supported ethics in American society and has contributed to its social ethics something like a full-fledged norm, order, or sense of direction, has now lost its power. I am sure that in the final analysis this is where the basic problem is to be located. Let me take this problem in a direction that deviates a little from the main theme. In the United States, the religious standpoint of Puritanism, which is the most severe of all the sects of Christianity, has prevailed. The essential feature of Puritanism—this term is, as is well known, derived from "pure" or "to purify"—lies in its pledge to purify Christianity, and to reactivate the Christian spirit, without making any compromise with worldly affairs. This Puritanism arose first of all in England. In the period when British society had been driven to utmost confusion, and various figures such as Cromwell had appeared on the scene, the way had been paved for a purified Christianity. There was once in England a period in which this Puritanism exerted great influence on politics and society. Confronted by reality, however, this Puritanism made a compromise. It was compelled to deal with the world by giving heed to various problems emerging from it.

This has something to do with the "skill in means" that Buddhism sets forth over against the truth. While the latter is permanent, reality undergoes constant change so that a variety of new problems arise. In an attempt to achieve permanent truth in reality, problems surface that cannot be solved through a pure standpoint whose essential feature lies in dealing with reality by relying on its own single-minded steadiness. Compromise makes its appearance here. But, even though compromise seems to be the result at the level of facts, when we delve further, we find that "skill in means" arises as an expedient to materialize the truth in reality.

This seems to be the reason why the relation between truth and "skill in means" has been treated in the theory of Buddhist doctrines as a difficult problem with which to cope. The basic point is that truth itself is realized through and through. Hence, it is held that "skill in means" is an artifact through which truth is realized in reality. Thus, it is thought to be a manifestation of the truth, if we pass judgment on it in the light of its basic spirit. And if we come to grips with this point fully, then "skill in means" turns out to be the truth; or rather, on the basis of this expedient, the truth is brought to realization with so much greater power. However this may be, as an expedient gradually gains in power, there appears the view that the expedient is not true after all, and that falsity is thus transformed into truth. I think it is not wrong to hold that falsity is temporarily recognized, with the expectation that the truth will thereby be realized subsequently. To take such a direction may be without fault. But there is involved in this Buddhist way of thinking a much greater danger. When doing so becomes an established custom, the spirit of truth tends to be lost sight of, and the result is that only the framework remains in place. Then falsity comes to the surface as an authentic falsity, with an ever strengthening potentiality. We cannot deny that this tendency appears in the development of history.

But I am sorry that my talk deviates from the main argument. Let us turn our attention to the case of America again. Confronted by reality, adherents of Puritanism—that is, of a very pure Christianity that had difficulty realizing its own aims in England—left England, where it had originated. The Puritans went to North America, and tried to build a new society in which to realize their own pure cause. This constituted the basis upon which the United States was established. For this reason, I am convinced that the history of the period in which this country was built, was carried out at a very high level and came to be known as the great experiment. I also feel that those who belonged to the early stage of Puritanism carried on their experiment at a very high level of idealism. But from the outset, there was a great problem that surfaced gradually in the history of America in a variety of forms.

In brief, the present situation is a degenerate age, resulting from the gradual loss of a Puritan tradition once held at a very high level.

This degenerate age is to be regarded as a stage on the way. The situation is similar to the Buddhist vision of the "true Law, the semblance Law, and the declining Law. This is evident were you to read a novel that was published a little while ago in America. The impression we get in New England, where Puritanism once had its age of glory, is that the upper classes came to believe that they had inherited the Puritan tradition. Most of them were Anglo-Saxons, whose level of knowledge was very high, and who supported America in its ritual and spiritual aspects, with a high self-confidence. They held the view that it was they who supported the financial power and economy of America and thus constituted the backbone of that country. It may be that Puritanism is still alive in the consciousness of these people. But I think that Puritanism, or rather the American spirit, is, in fact, not embodied in them. It is not the case that spirit becomes flesh to the extent that it constitutes their very personality. Instead, they are deprived of spirit, so that only the frame is left.

To speak in terms of Buddhist doctrine, in the days of the Law there was "testimony." I do not know exactly what "testimony" is, but we can presumably identify it with what I have just said in terms of spirit—that is, spirit is embodied so as to constitute a human being. In the process through which some person achieves the status of genuine human being, the spirit of Buddha's Law (if we are here allowed to refer to Buddhism) is at work as a power enabling a human being to be a human being in the genuine sense. In other words, if we suppose that the spirit is the forming principle of a human being, then the spirit of Buddha's Law makes its appearance by becoming a human being. To use a term derived from the West, what we are concerned with here is the "incarnation" of spirit through which spirit comes forth by becoming a living human body. This is what is meant by "testimony."

I think that "testimony" is not recognizable in the present upper classes in America. For they practice their spirituality only in a formal way. Here only its frame is left. This is why I use the Buddhist term "the semblance Law" to describe such practice. I have the strong impression that they are proud of the Puritan tradition, and are very haughty in manner. What remains, however, is only the tradition that has come down from former times. I think that this tradition is almost impotent to make them into human beings in the genuine sense. They are accustomed and taught to carry on their lives in accordance with this tradition, and always have a consciousness of it. That is the reason why they have a very high opinion of themselves and a certain pride. However this may be, the fact is that what remains is only the frame, but not the spirit. Therefore, even though they impress those who happen to come from the outside with their high-mindedness, I cannot erase the impression that out of their practice of acting and living, a spiritual void comes forth and that they are certainly richly dressed but shabby in spirit. I have gleaned from farmers and workers in that county that they are more simple in manner and behavior than the upper classes.

So far as the general situation in America at present is concerned, it is now far worse, and is devoid of both frame and power. Sometimes this situation is thought of as ridiculous by most of the younger generation. This is why they sometimes have a desire to break all of these things to pieces. For instance, those who are called "hippies" seem to have a strong antipathy toward this deceitful spiritual posture, where only the frame remains intact. So then: America made its start from a purity-oriented ideology at a very high level—so high that we get the impression that its corruption is a cause for far more misery than in Europe. This is the reason why there has arisen among young people in America an interest in the Buddhism of Tibet, India, and Japan. America is now in such a special situation.

The Kingdom of God

I am sorry that my talk has diverged from the main theme. My point is that the collapse of the family in America is disclosed in the phenomenon of divorce, and that the breakdown of teachings inherent in Puritanism and Christianity lurks behind the collapse of family ethics, inherited from Puritanism. This means that the history of America is corrupt at its spiritual foundation. I think that this is a most crucial problem. Politics and economics in America are of course problematical. But the fact is that together with Christianity, which is the prevalent religion, the traditions of ethics and of mind, and the kind of thought and truth in which people have had confidence, have now broken down. It is quite difficult to rehabilitate the original position. Unless this difficult problem is resolved, I am afraid that something like a large-scale earthquake, in which the foundation itself is threatened, will occur again and again.

The issue of the family is a crucial one, and is concerned with social problems in general. Adults and even children seem to enjoy a great degree of freedom concerning divorce. But in truth, I am sure that men and women are aware of a dark side at the bottom of their hearts. At any rate, what is at stake is the question concerning a human being, as well as the question concerning the power of religion, which has exerted its influence upon social life under the guise of ethics. That in which we human beings put our faith, and through which we are enabled to say that this is certain or that is false—the most basic issue by virtue of which we are able to live—is now threatened and is already wavering.

The problem of ethics is not limited to the affairs of the family, but also extends to the international relations between countries, which are also a very complicated matter. International problems, such as North-South affairs, are of a scale greater than family affairs, and have to do with such issues as the control of nuclear weapons, which threaten the destiny of mankind as a whole if we are not careful in handling them. Here in Japan, there is a tendency for us to be ridiculed if we dare to speak of patriotism. But in reality, we cannot dispose of it so simply as is usually supposed. At any rate, the most positive meaning of a country consists in "blood and land," just as the National Socialist Party in Germany had insisted on *Blut und Boden* when they tried to think of their country. But blood relations and the land in the sense of the land of the country must be dealt with as crucial issues. On the one hand, they are tied up with something like karma taken in the bad sense, but the issues are also connected with the life of a human being, and with the importance that blood relations have in our lives. The term "land" refers not only to the physical soil, but also to a kind of symbol. That is to say, it is regarded as the rock foundation that gives birth to and supports all things, rendering them capable of taking root and growing up. The term "country" has the same characteristics. To extend our argument, we can say that it is the land of God. We think of the land as a symbol of the country, and by enlarging it all the way to God, we are able to speak of "the Kingdom of God." Be this as it may, what we are now considering are the land, the land of God, and the Buddha's land or the Pure Land. They are all quite basic lands. The next crucial question to ask is what they signify.

The Buddhist Concept of "Karma"

I have strayed from the subject of conscience. But since I am here concerned with ethics, it is perhaps natural that my talk does not make such progress as you might expect. Why do I raise this question about the land? Because the land is connected with sentient beings, and with human beings in particular. It is not only that sentient beings are living, but rather that they are allowed to live. They are living by being allowed to live. Regarding the deepest ground of one's living, it is not the case that one exists merely by one's own free will. And it is inevitable that the problem of others also arises. What is at stake are the relations between a husband and a wife, parents and children, and the self and others, if we extend our argument to human relations in general. It is only in and through the basic structures by virtue of which the self cannot be separated from others that a human being can be adequately conceived.

The fundamental reason why the land draws special attention in the midst of these relations is that human beings, who come into being in such a way as to be in inseparable relationships with others are conceived of as based upon a comprehensive standpoint that is inclusive of themselves and others as well, and in it they are all allowed to live. If we advance to the ground of our living, the view must be maintained that we are living while being allowed to do so. This is the reason why the self and others are inseparable. But in this case, we must also say that others render it possible for the self to live.

If we grant the fact that we are allowed to live, then many things thereby must be taken into consideration. Basically speaking, gods and Buddhas must now be considered. But at the same time, they must be considered in connection with the land. For instance, in Christianity, the Kingdom of God is spoken of. Here God and a human being are connected in a way that involves the land under the guise of a kingdom. So far as the Kingdom of God is concerned, we are tempted to say that something smelling of mud makes the picture fade. Despite this fact, and keeping an eye on the basic significance of the land, we must say that human beings are born from it, take root there, and, fundamentally grow by taking advantage of it as a foothold. We can assert that, fundamentally, individuals come to be connected with each other through the medium of the land.

For example, grass and trees cannot come into existence only by themselves. Basically, they go into the ground, and then there is a process through which the ground and the end of their root come to be united. This most basic form is delicate in its characteristics. There is here a distinction and, at the same time, there is communication. There is a borderline and yet at the same time interconnection. This basic form plays a role as a kind of membrane. A membrane both lets something in and shuts something out. I find here such an inherently mysterious relationship. A blade of grass or a tree takes root in this ground and forms a living connection with it. Here is the basic form by means of which it draws up water and transforms it into its living power, enabling its branches to shoot out and its flowers to come into bloom. In the relationship between the root and the land there is involved the fact that to live is to be allowed to live. And at the same time, the fact that it is allowed to live turns out to be the power through which it endeavors to live. These two things are here united into one. Thus, through the soil there arises the great comprehensive power in all things—that is, the power of nature itself. In the case of a human being, the land of the country, or the country itself, is the focal point.

At any rate, my view is that, when we are allowed to live, the land is always under consideration. Therefore, even when reference is made not only to the nation constructed by human beings but also to the Kingdom of God, something like the land is envisioned. Even with reference to Buddhas, it is symbolically said that sentient beings are born in the country of Buddhas, where they become tied to Buddhas. This renders their relationship with Buddhas a living one. I think that it is here that the meaning of the the country of Buddhas comes into question.

Some complicated problems arise, however, in particular the problem of what the relationship is between the Pure Land and this impure one, or what the term *sive* means when mention is made of "the corrupt and vile world *sive* the land of serene light." Even though it is possible to hold various opinions about this, I am convinced that the land is at the bottom of them all. The land still comes into consideration when we think of a country from a worldly standpoint, to say nothing of the world of religions. There is also the question of blood relations, as well as our relation to the land.

Here problems arise one after another. If reference is made to culture, such as the Japanese culture, to politics, economics, and, in brief, to the concrete history of human beings, what is usually referred to as a country appears as having great relevance. Such a state of affairs is involved in determining the direction of history. Even though the necessity for moving away from this direction may arise in the remote future, it seems to be a difficult task to accomplish for the time being. In the final analysis, this difficulty has something to do with karma or nature. Karma, in the bad sense of the word, allures human beings to wage wars and destroy each other. The ruling powers also come to the surface. These things are, after all, directly related to the karma lying at the foundation of a country. But there is good aspect to this same karma. There is the possibility that these two aspects of karma may both come to the fore, when a human being is said to be allowed to live.

In brief, karma, taken in the broad sense of the word, constitutes the root of a human being—that is, it exists as the basis of human life. And individual human beings are impotent to dispose of this karma.

Karma cannot be identified with the simple notion of fate. That human beings are allowed to live cannot truly be understood unless it is connected with the fact that they endeavor to live. If we do not conceive of the fact that we are allowed to live our life through our endevoring to live, we fall victim to a kind of fatalism. If we keep an eye on the fact that we endeavor to live, light is shed on such things as freedom and will as being of great importance. And judging from the fact that we are allowed to live, we cannot simply dispose of this fact as we please. Here we must consider that which is called necessity. In this way, freedom and necessity are united into one. Necessity lies at the very bottom of freedom. But this necessity is not mere fate. Rather, we must think that it is necessity in the sense that it is at the very bottom of freedom. Otherwise we could not conceive of the meaning of karma. Karma is concerned with ethics in this way: insofar as it is connected with freedom or will, it becomes entangled with the issues of good and bad.

The Confucianist Dictum "Heaven Knows" is Related to a Great Disclosure

Let us now raise the question of what the significance of conscience is in the context of an ethical problem. The activity of conscience as manifest in "conscience reproach," has to do with the deepest recesses of each individual. Every individual has a hidden room belonging to him or her alone, and into which nobody else can peep. That conscience reproaches signifies that there is within everyone an area accessible to him or her alone, and that one alone blames oneself in secret while nobody else can know this. This reproach of conscience is not known to anyone else insofar as our social life is concerned. But in relationship to others as well as to society, each individual possesses something that steps outside this relationship. Here lies the genuine standpoint of the individual. This means that there is "my" standpoint over against the public one. It is in this private realm that conscience reproaches.

Let us take the profession of carpenter as an illustration. In the social relations based on social function, a carpenter makes it his own business to build a house. After building it, he receives money. For a genuine carpenter, the question of whether or not he is content with the house he has built remains to be dealt with. Even though the house is evaluated by others as well constructed, it may be that he cannot experience full-fledged satisfaction from it, from his standpoint as an artisan. In this case, the social function is so well performed at the public level that there is no problem legally, in terms of social ethics. In spite of this, there is the possibility that the standpoint of an artisan as carpenter leaves him dissatisfied. What is left troubled is his conscience. If he feels, without knowing why, that his conscience bothers him, a conscientious carpenter continues to do his work until it eventually satisfies him. This continuation of his work has nothing to do with the issue of law or his promises to society. If he carries on his work to his satisfaction, then the reproach of conscience disappears, and he is likely to confirm this by saying that this is enough—that is, he stands on the position that he has complied with his own intentions.

Here he reaches himself, and has the feeling that he treads on the soil. There is no difference between his saying yes to himself and to the house. Since the truly ought-to-be-house is built, we can say that it is brought to completion as a house in the authentic sense of the word. Indeed, for a sincere and conscientious carpenter there is no difference between the house and himself. By his becoming himself, he can say yes in a calm manner. This is identical with the fact that the house becomes a house itself. If someone wishes to see him, this carpenter is able to say, "Look at this house." It is established in conscience that he is one with the house and the house is one with him.

It is on this conscientiousness that the most fundamental affairs in human relationships are based. Yet the question remains: in the case of an artisan, on what basis does his work arise? Here the question is whether authentic human relations are in fact based on conscience. And this question is to be answered in the affirmative. What makes its appearance here is the private reserve called "mine," to which no one else has access.

There is one more question to be raised in connection with conscience: the question of whether conscience is said to be like a secret room because it is concerned only with what is "mine." As a matter of fact, this is not so. With regard to conscience, to borrow terminology peculiar to Confucianism, we can say that "Heaven knows and the earth also knows," despite the fact that nobody else knows. To speak of this matter in an existential fashion, "Heaven" here refers to the religious dimension. Even though I spoke earlier about a secret room, it is rather an opening toward heaven. While that which reproaches me has to do not with affairs that are affiliated with social publicity, inclusive of laws and so forth, but with individual and private affairs affiliated with this secret room, in reality it stands amid the great light. Here the term "light" refers to the dictum that "Heaven knows." For this reason, that conscience reproaches me means that I am made to stand in front of something great such as heaven and earth. The phrase "something great" also refers to what is inclusive of me, which was suggested by the above-mentioned dictum that I am living while being allowed to do so. To speak in a manner characteristic of Confucianism, the dictum that "Heaven knows and the earth also knows" means that the secret room is opened up toward a public that is higher than the limited publicity called society, which human beings have mutually constructed and which even goes beyond the nation and humankind. This higher public Confucianism tries to describe in terms of heaven and earth. It goes without saying that this public has a religious implication. In the West, the phrase "before God" refers to this higher public. I am quite sure that this is the most crucial point to be kept in mind.

As regards the "work" of the artisan, my argument asserts that it is conceived at the place where heaven and a human being are related to each other. The same idea is available in the West. Max Weber made clear in his theories of the artisan that a *Beruf* (calling) was in Protestantism regarded as a gift from heaven. This means that they pushed their own works to the fullness demanded, and went as far as the problem of conscience itself.

Let us again refer to the carpenter as our illustration. It is because his work is still left unfinished that his conscience reproaches him. His work is left unfinished in relation not only to others but also to himself. This is what is implied by the Japanese word *sumanai*. What is suggested is that all these "things" are left unfinished. It is conscience that informs us of this fact most clearly. We are here hampered from settling down to, and feeling at home with, ourselves.

What is the meaning of "confession?" When conscience reproaches us, we are said to "confess." In this case, conscience has to do with the voice of heaven. Despite the fact that many things are hidden from others, I myself know them. Even though others may not know them, heaven knows them. In this way, *Beruf* is to be conceived of as occurring not so much at the place where we are said to be allowed to live, but rather at the place where we are said to be gifted.

The Path Peculiar to Workers

Ancient people speak of their *inochi* (life) as ordered. Here the word "order" has nothing to do with "influence exerted from above." It is certainly by their own choice, but nevertheless, it is something "ordered," to speak of this in a fundamental way. The term "life" implies that we are ordered to do something beyond that which we have decided to do. This is the order that is implied in the phrase "an ordered task." At the bottom of our living lies such an "order." We push our existence to its consequence and try to become ourselves through living in compliance with conscience. As a result, we feel at home with ourselves. This state of mind is called *anshinritsumei* in Japanese; its literal meaning is that our mind settles down to itself, so that our life comes to be firmly established.

The life that we have in mind when we say that our mind is truly calm and tranquil is the life I just mentioned. In this life, we say that, while being allowed to live, we are living. It is for this reason that an authentic work becomes an ordered task. While it is the path along which we live our lives, it has the characteristic of genuine order. This notion of order is derived from Confucianism. In the path of heaven, and of a human being, truthfulness is at stake. The Chinese character that is here translated as "truthfulness" is *makoto* in Japanese. It means in China that "something has been accomplished." The term *makoto* implies that when human beings try to live an authentic life, which is not contrived by them at their own pleasure, a great direction comes to be recognized. At the base of *makoto* lies the view that there is a path for a human being that renders it possible to truly realize heaven's order and to transform it into *makoto*.

Then what is this truth or truthfulness? As something different from the truth of scientific knowledge, it comes to light in the depths of human existence. For this reason, it comes forth as an issue of conscience, at the bottom of which the meaning inherent in our religious life is revealed. What has so far been said is connected with ethics. I think that the issue of conscience comes to the fore at various places as well.

For instance, students in Japan are now killing each other because of the internal struggles of the student movement. I think that this is quite a silly thing indeed. I am sure that they stop far short of conscience. Of course, they try to justify themselves though they attempt to purify their position through self-reflection, I think that belligerent atheism lurks behind their thought. They endeavor to fully justify their fighting, and to purify it by wiping out impure elements, so that the basic position of their struggle may be distinctly established. Such a development is possible, only if belligerent atheism is pushed to its conclusion. However different in form, this development also makes its appearance in religion in the West. It is a kind of Puritanism. It is in many respects similar to conscience in thoroughly purifying its own position. It has something in common with the direction taken by conscience in its attempt to search for a direction that enables those who are engaged in the struggle to say within themselves that this is exactly the cause to fight for. Therefore, they do not worry about the criticisms other people level against them. The reason lies, I think, in their conviction that, so far as their cause is concerned, these criticisms are beside the mark. However, this is something different from conscience.

Then what is the point which makes this version of Puritanism differ from conscience? It differs in falling short of the dictum: "Heaven knows and the earth knows," and further, in the respect that there is no room for this dictum to intervene here. Unlike the artisan, when these students insist on breaking down present society and opening the door to a new society they are, frankly speaking, devoid of the awareness that a human being is living by being allowed to do so, as has been taught in religions from ancient times. For this reason, no matter how often they speak of conscience, they try, after all, to appeal to it at the place where genuine human relations do not come forward. The issue of conscience is tied up with that of religion, as was said before, in which deed, faith, and testimony are all involved.

In brief, if we speak of truthfulness in the case of a carpenter, we can say that the relationship between him and the others is so deep that he is totally trustworthy. He is relied upon as a human being, irrespective of whether or not he fulfilled his own promises according to the contract. Thus far, this is related to the problem of mind. With reference to his deeds or works, we can rely on them and on what he says. The distinction has long been made between mind, body, and speech. So far as trust is concerned, it appears in many forms; one may rely on the carpenter's works as well as on what he says, and leave everything to his decision. But the basis is, after all, conscience. At the same time, the depth of one's conscience consists in one's knowing heaven and earth so that it paves the way to the path that an artisan should take. Walking along this path, workers are engaged in doing their job in compliance with conscience, with the result that they rectify themselves in the process. In Confucianism, it is called a divinely ordered task, and turns out eventually to be a concern of religion. Therefore there are many gods—for instance, a god of artisans, a god of musicians, and so forth. Faith is involved here. More fundamental even than this, in the cases of Christianity and Buddhism, there appears the heavenly ordered task, or the order from God, when we face Buddha or God. This is trust, or faith. Here again conscience is involved, in connection with which we say that conscience reproaches us, or that we have an awareness that we have left something unfinished. This is the case not only with the Pure Land gate of Buddhism, but also with the Sacred Path gate. But I would like to reserve our discussion of Buddhism for tomorrow's talk.

6

To Make Sure of Oneself

Religion is Intimately Connected with the Privacy of a Human Being

Yesterday, I spoke about conscience. My point was that what appears as conscience in the modern age surfaces as an issue of ethics, in the broad sense of the word, and that ethics involves within itself problems that ethics itself cannot adequately handle. The most important of these problems is that ethics, while tentatively distinguished from religion, is somehow still connected with it. Hence, in an attempt to conceive of conscience, I think it more appropriate to take ethics into consideration from a broader context, rather than to consider it in the narrow sense alone. Another theme, which I discussed yesterday, was that conscience, if taken in its broad sense, is connected with ethics, but that at the same time, it is involved in almost all other problems as well. Wang Yang-ming himself seems to have grasped conscience in such a broad sense. As I said yesterday, in the midst of activities through which a worker produces things, there inevitably arise relations between him and other persons. For instance, when he builds a house or produces pottery, there must be some who are in need of such things, and buy them, since they are necessities of life. In other words, "to produce something" is made possible only by presupposing the existence of its counterparts in society—that is, production is made possible only in and through the resultant social relationships with others. It is all right to describe this relation in terms of "social relations," or to take a different viewpoint, in terms of "human relations." Among these social relations, the problem of self, in addition to the human relations we have with other persons, constitutes a very important factor. The point of my talk yesterday was to insist that it would not be too much to say that social relations pivot on the problem of the self.

131

Since that which is public and social appears in social relations at a place where communal life is carried on, it has the characteristic of being "common." The term "common" suggests that the self and others have something in common, on the basis of which society is established. This is the reason why a society is often called a community. It has the quality of *ōyake* (the public). In distinction from such a society, the term *watakushi* (privacy) is used. As reference is often made to *kōshikondō* (to mix up public and private matters), these terms are frequently used as opposite concepts, but at the same time, as united.

The private side consists of what belongs to an individual himself or herself, and is incommensurable with that of others. It tells us of a way of being human beings in which we are left to ourselves alone. We cannot conceive of human beings apart from this private side in which we have our own individual way of being incommensurable with others. At the bottom of this private side, called "mine," there remains something intact concerning which "I" differs from everyone else. Needless to say, this aspect makes its appearance in various places, and plays quite important roles in various forms.

Zen Buddhism attaches great importance to this aspect. Among a variety of stories concerned with dreams that were once told, let me choose the following one. In ancient times, a monk was told by his master to go on an errand. It took him many days to reach another monk living in a far-off temple. The first monk was a serious-minded man, and before leaving he had complained about the master's order, saying that he was at a loss about what to do because he had wanted to devote much of his time to more discipline and sitting meditation. Hearing the complaint, a senior fellow monk said he would go with him, and together they had set out. On their way, this senior disciple said to him, "I would like to do many things on your behalf. But there are things that I cannot do in your place." In saying this, he had in mind such things as urination, defecation, and sleep. Concerning them, the story goes, he said to his junior disciple, "By all means, you should do them."

This private aspect seems to be of great importance. Things which we can by no means ask others to do on our behalf do not belong to the public domain. There are many such things in our daily life. In fact, they lurk in the background of almost all aspects of life. The moral of the above story is that after all, no matter how many times you take a trip, or how much you wander around outside of the temple, Zen Buddhist discipline cannot be exhausted by what we do only within the temple, and things such as sleep and going to the toilet all exist in the same field of discipline. The reason why these things have meaning in the field of discipline is that these are activities in which each of us cannot be replaced by others, and through which we are genuinely able to come back to ourselves. What is at issue here has something to do with enlightenment, since what is now under consideration is Zen Buddhism. I am sure that enlightenment is only achieved on the basis of our coming back to ourselves. However much you may recite sūtras, all of your efforts are of no use, unless you occupy the place called "yours," with respect to which you cannot be replaced by others. Hearing his senior disciple saying that, the monk decided to go on the errand alone.

The Threefold Relationship in Which a Thing is in Relation to Itself, the Self Relates Itself to Itself, and the Self and Others are Related to Each Other

In this way, everyone possesses something that is not susceptible to being replaced by others. In comparison with the relation between self and others, it can be said to consist in the way in which the self is related to itself. These two kinds of relations combine to give birth to generally accepted social ideas and to the public side of a society, in which there are various systems such as laws, power politics, social organizations, and so forth. This is a state of affairs that is inevitably required in order for a society to exist. No matter how much a society undergoes transformation, we cannot conceive of it apart from its organization, or apart from its social systems. Except anarchism, which has no social organizations, power politics inevitably arises, as well as the relations between superiors and inferiors, the rulers and the ruled. Indeed, social structure and social system cannot be established apart from them.

However this may be, at the root of social and human relations there lurks the fact that each person is his own individual, and that the relation that he bears to himself at the place beyond the standpoint called "common" is a place where nobody can be replaced by another. This position alone enables each one to be himself, and at the same time renders genuine human relations capable of being established.

In this sense, what is called a social relation is accompanied by an aspect that is transcendent to the so-called social. It is this aspect which supports social relations at their basis, and from which everyone goes back to his basic individuality and where each and every one is related to himself as his own individual. This is exactly what is constituted by the relationship between one human being and another. At bottom, there is the relation that is truly "mine," as I said before, and it is through it that social relations—that is, objective matters of fact such as institutions and organizations—are rendered possible. I think it appropriate to describe the relation of the self to itself, which is characteristic of Kierkegaard's thought, in terms of "subjectivity." What is required of each person is to make his own subjectivity clear to himself. It is only through one's standing on one's own subjectivity that objective social systems are supported. I think that such an idea holds true here.

In the example of the carpenter, which was used yesterday, it was made clear that even something that is no problem socially can leave one feeling, in one's self-awareness, that things are still unfinished. Because of this, one is obliged to pursue them further, and by doing so, one returns back to oneself, and uses up oneself in doing. Only then will the carpenter feel at home with himself, and become composed. Otherwise, he will experience a constant sense of anxiety. By realizing that some unfinished things were finally brought to completion, the relation between self and others is thereby rendered capable of being a genuine relationship.

At the same time, that which was thus produced turns out to be the house itself. The three things in this relationship—in which a thing is related to itself, and in which the self relates itself to itself and finally, the self and others are related to one another as human beings—are all simultaneously established as one. And there arises the authentic truthfulness in which a thing returns back to the place where it ought to be, and in which the self realizes itself, and thus returns to and settles down in the place where it ought to be.

At the same time, judging from the activity, we can say that a thing is produced and is realized just as a thing, and that the self also comes to be realized in an authentic way. Only then is the relation between the self and others materialized in its authentic form.

Regress *sive* Progress

To describe this in a wider context, the aforementioned threefold relationship comes into being and is renewed in a temporal fashion, time and time again. What makes its appearance here, to put it grandly, is the basic form of history, in which a human being's mode of existence is seen as historical. But at the same time, this basic form of history has another sense in which we turn back, step by step, to what we ought to be. From this, it is fair to say that, while something new is always realized on each occasion of human existence, this renewed realization is always made possible by something basically unchangeable, and in such a way that human existence is brought back to this unchangeable, and thus settles down in the place where it ought to do so. To speak of the matter differently: while treading on the same spot, we constantly go on a walk, and thus we always take a new step forward. What this means is that, while continuing to take a new step forward, we simultaneously tread on the same spot, right under our feet. The phrase "to tread on the same spot" is here used in such a sense that it holds true, if we were to pass judgment on the matter from the most fundamental standpoint. The term "fundamental standpoint" is meant to refer to the manner in which we are said to be allowed to, or are made to live, as I remarked earlier. As to this, we can say that, if we judge from the origin of human existence, then there is no change, or that we tread on the same spot. Nevertheless, while treading on the same spot, we do in fact go onward, walking step by step, if we judge from the fact that something new is realized. And if the constant walking is held in view, it is related to the testimony which we bear to the Buddhist truth through deed, that is, deed-testimony. The Japanese phrase *fuekiryūkō* describes this. *Fueki* means "no change," while *ryūkō* literally means "fashionableness"— that is, "not staying on the same spot even for a moment and thus undergoing constant change." Therefore, this Japanese phrase means that, while we are involved in constant change, there is no change, as far as Buddhist truth is concerned, to which we bear testimony through our deeds.

We encounter this sort of situation everywhere, which means that progress is at the same time regress. To return to the origin, in the true sense, is to advance forward. That is to say, our constant creation of novelty is fundamentally made possible only by our standing on something unchangeable. The term "unchangeable" is here meant to refer to the creative power, which is the source from which the enlivening power gushes. The unchangeable has to do with the source of this spring of life and creation.

In the discourses of Confucius, mention is frequently made that "water incessantly gushes out from the fountainhead." I think that Confucius was pointing here to something similar to what I have just mentioned. Such a fountainhead lurks at the bottom of human existence, that bottom in which we are ourselves alone, and not replaceable by anyone else. At the source of the life of a human being, no matter whether one moves one's body or says something, there is that which permeates everything, for a human being's karma is at work through one's behavior as a whole, as is made evident in the Buddhist phrase "the threefold karma of body, speech, and mind." The word "karma" here refers to the source of a human being. In order that this source may exercise such power, it must be that we return to ourselves so that we may exist there just as we are; at the same time, this source is led to a great disclosure in which it is said that "Heaven knows and the earth also knows." This dimension of human relationship is rather like a secret room, and we can say of this source that it is not understandable to anybody else. The same can be said of everyone. In ancient times, reference was made to *reidanjichi*, which means that it is through the knowledge acquired by one's self—that is, through one's drinking water by oneself that one comes to know whether it is hot or cold. I think that this point is of great importance. What is under consideration here is something that presents itself very much like a secret room.

Conscience is much the same. It is to be found at some hidden place within each human being, where such things occur as the awareness that "my conscience pricks me," or that "my conscience is brought to satisfaction," or that " I am not ashamed of my conscience." But this is not the whole story. The reason why conscience is able to possess meaning as conscience is that it is also at the same time opened up toward a great and absolute disclosure that is more appropriate to describe in terms of heaven and earth, and that is different from the public found in the human world. It is only here that we are made to be, or where we live by being allowed to live. Here a double structure seems to appear. But in reality, it is not double but united.

As to this point, a little while ago I provisionally enumerated four relations. Firstly, there is the relation the self bears to itself; secondly, there is the relation between it and a thing, or to say this more straightforwardly, the relation that a thing bears to itself. Thirdly, there is the relation between the self and others; and fourthly, there is the relation of the self with the Absolute. And these four relations simultaneously arise as united into one. My point is that it is here that conscience is truly taken into account.

We are then led to the conclusion that ethics—that is, those human relationships which are thought of as the ethical—comes to be of great importance, and is, at the same time, related to something Absolute. The term "Absolute" is here meant to refer to what allows all things to be or to live. If we keep an eye on what is allowed to be, that which allows all things to be has the meaning of the Absolute. These relations, inclusive of that to the Absolute, combine to make it possible for us to conceive of conscience fully.

It is in connection with this problem that Shinran, the founder of the Pure Land sect of Buddhism, is to be considered. In his thought, the problem of conscience is tied up with such problems as faith, deed-testimony, and so forth. Concerning the structure of conscience, the case is the same with this-worldly affairs.

Consciousness and Conscience

Earlier, I referred to the old meaning of the word *ryōshin* ("good mind," conscience), of which we make use nowadays in Japan, but which originated in China. However, the meaning we attribute to it today is derived from the Western word "conscience." When we say that my *ryōshin* reproaches me, the term *ryōshin* is used in this modern sense. The original word "conscience" consists of two components; "con" and "science." "Con" indicates a gathering of all things together, and thus refers to the person as a whole, and the original meaning of "science" is "knowledge." "Con" has to do with that which is all-inclusive, which consists not so much in all things collected one by one as in the whole that is given birth when these things are brought together. Thus, the "con" gives expression to the whole as such. It is because of the fact that all things are united at their basis and thus constitute the whole that the collecting of them one by one is rendered possible. The word "con" is used to imply the whole in its flow, in which things come into being as united into one of their own accord, rather than as gathered by a human being. They are originally established all together, or are united into one. The four relations come into being as connected into one. The first relation is that one always relates oneself to oneself. The second is the relation of the self to other things. The third is the relation of the self to other persons. And the fourth consists in there being something that supports the self, others, and things as a whole. These relations, including that to something great and absolute, are united into one.

As I mentioned, "science" is concerned with knowledge and the means "to know." At the background of knowledge thus established lies the fact that the self knows itself when it returns to itself. When it is said that we feel relieved, and settle down to ourselves, this means that we have returned to ourselves. And this involves within itself a kind of self-knowledge through which the self knows what it really is like. This self-knowledge exists at the very bottom of each individual. Such knowledge involves self-consciousness within itself. In this case, reference is made to self-consciousness. The word "conscious" is related to "conscience," and includes, after all, an implication of knowing. What is at stake here is something very subjective, through which the self constantly becomes conscious of itself as an individual.

The "self-consciousness" that I have in mind, however, is used to denote not so much the self-consciousness that is meant when we say that someone strongly adheres to his or her self-consciousness, but rather the fact that the self exists. Self-consciousness of this sort is concerned not so much with the fact that each individual enters into its own interior, and comes into contact with nothing but itself. Rather, it involves within itself the fact that the self truly knows itself, and that this self-knowledge is at the same time accompanied by some sort of activity.

What is under consideration here is a knowledge that is simultaneously connected with the deed through which we produce something. It is somewhat equivalent to the ancient Japanese term *yū,* used in its broad sense. This is a standpoint in which knowledge and deed are united into one. Let us take up the carpenter again as our illustration. Through his activity of building a house, he proceeds truly to become himself, or rather truly to build himself. It is only through the building of a house that his existence is brought to self-consciousness, and thereby he comes to know himself. For this reason, he is liable to tell others to look at the house he built if they want to know him. In this case, he is identified with the house. Therefore, we can say that he comes to know himself in and through this activity. This is somewhat different from self-centered consciousness.

The essential feature of the latter sort of self-consciousness lies in the fact that the self becomes conscious of itself as always centered around itself. But the sort of self-consciousness I have in mind is at work outside the self, even without being conscious of its activity, reaching toward the outside. Here the self gets out of itself, and engages itself in activities out there—for instance, in gathering brushwood and giving orders to one's disciples in the midst of one's concern for other things. What is at stake here is human existence itself, because the essential meaning of the term "existence" is to stand out of oneself. Here the way is paved for us to come to know our own existence at the place where we get out into the world of things, and into relations with other people.

In an attempt to conceive of the self, however, we used to hold the view that there is what is called a thing, or another person, to which we relate ourselves. This is the view that the self exists somewhere alone in separation from others, whenever one speaks of the subject-object relation. The self is conceived of as surrounded by various other things. From ancient times, this standpoint has been called the consciousness of discrimination. But this is not a truly living form of existence. Indeed, it has nothing to do with the life that we are in fact living. It falls victim to self-centered consciousness. That we actually live our life cannot be conceived of apart from the fact that we live together with others.

Therefore, for us to be together with other persons does not mean that our house is presupposed, and then we get out of it. Instead of conceiving of our "self" as getting out of our house from the outset, we conceive of it *here* in the midst of our concerns with others. This is exactly what is meant by the Japanese *jitafuni*, which means that the self and others cannot be separated from each other.

Self-consciousness is the Place in which the Basic Relationship between One Human Being and Another Occurs

According to the modern way of thinking, the self is ego-like. But the authentic self cannot be conceived of by means of this paradigm. Let us take as an example a worker who performs his duties precisely and rigidly in producing a teacup. If he conscientiously strives to achieve what he set out to achieve, then the question of what he is stands out in sharp relief. This is what the Japanese word *koto* refers to. He is engaged in his *koto*, which is work understood in its broadest sense, in order to do and to achieve something. In this something is involved his self, other people, other things, and, more fundamentally speaking, something greater than all of them. The Japanese word *koto* is very ambiguous in its implications. In English, when we have in mind some important matter of fact, the term "cause" is used. The Japanese word *koto* has something to do with one's country, as when we busy ourselves with that which concerns our country. We cannot dispose of this matter of our country in a simple business-like manner. Rather, we are immersed in it, and become one with it. What comes to the fore here is that whole which is called one's country, and which is inclusive of other things and other persons. In reality, this state of affairs exists everywhere. If we put it into English, I am sure that the word "cause" hits the mark.

In Latin, it is *res*, which is equivalent to the aforementioned *koto*. The term "republic" is derived from *res publica*. It is here that the self, as well as "to know," are established.

What we are now considering is not self-consciousness, but rather self-awareness. The latter is concerned with the problem of how the self truly comes to know itself. By contrast, since everyone in ordinary self-consciousness becomes conscious of his or her own self, the question of how the self comes to know itself does not really arise here. In the worst case, a strongly egoistic tendency surfaces. Therefore, the standpoint of self-consciousness is rather a standpoint in which the self is captured for itself. And concerning this, I have the impression that here the self confines itself within a narrow prison. But this is not a basic feature of the existence of the self.

In order to give expression to this authentic standpoint in English, we should say: "I am." This sentence expresses the subjective mode of a human being. This subjective mode is, in truth, established on the basis of its relation with things. In other words, it is established not as a mode closed within itself, but at a place about which we must say that it was out there from the outset—that is, at a place beyond the distinction between inside and outside, a place about which it has been said from ancient times that we are beyond the distinction between subject and object. This mode of being human is nothing less than self-awareness. In this case, the self turns out truly to be itself, and is established as being at one with the fact that it is a thing that truly turns out to be itself. And the manner in which a thing turns out to be itself is one in which the self and a thing are brought to self-awareness as united into one. As I said before, we are able to say here that "This house is my self," and to ask others to look at it when we want to show ourselves to others. In this sense, there is a likelihood of our coming to know ourselves through producing a thing.

If this is truly the case in our relations with other things, then we can also say this with respect to the relations between one human being and another, if we come to know each other in the true sense of the word. That we become truly acquainted with a friend means not that we know only his or her name, but that we come into contact with his or her conscience. In compliance with the demands of conscience, we are honest and true to ourselves, and do not deceive ourselves. It is only when I truly know others as conscientious persons that trust arises. That we are true and honest with ourselves means that we have precise knowledge of our defects, try to overcome them, and strive to reach a place from which we are able to say that this is all right. This is exactly what is meant by saying that we are honest with ourselves.

There is no difference between saying that we are honest about our work and saying that we are honest with ourselves. It is due to this fact alone that we are able to trust others. That is to say, human relations are established on the basis of trust in this sense. This trust consists in each individual human being striving to be honest with herself or himself. It was with this in view that I referred to "mind" yesterday. Only then is the relation between human beings truly established, for now they truly come to be acquainted with each other. The term "with" indicates that we have come to trust each other in the true sense. In this "trust" is involved the fact that we are supported by others, or that we have come to rely on them.

The relation between the self and others consists in this mutual support. This does not mean that they help each other with respect to matters that are of little or no value, but that they depend on each other in those basic relationships between one human being and another. This mutual dependence is truly possible on condition that each of them is absolutely independent or, perhaps I should say, that the person does not leave himself or herself entirely to the care of others or takes advantage of another person's kindness. This is because both money and social status fall short of rendering a human being capable of genuinely being himself or herself, and if this is so, then we must strive to overcome this state of affairs. Only in this way is one able to be true to oneself. I am sure that this situation obtains only when one is firmly rooted in a standpoint of independence. It is an authentic subjectivity that renders trust possible. Only a human being who is truthful is deemed trustworthy by others. This is nothing less than the mutuality of interdependent relations. It might be the case that those who are deprived of their independence and are in trouble come to help each other. This may be all right. But in most of these cases, when something goes wrong with a relationship based on self-interest, it is ordinarily taken for granted that it breaks down immediately. But since what is now being considered is the basic relation between one human being and another, when the self truly relates itself to itself, then this self-relation simultaneously renders possible a true relationship between the self and others. The Japanese word equivalent to the English word "friend" is *tomodachi. Tomo* means "with." The emphasis is on a togetherness with others through which human beings actually come together. This is the essential feature of a human being. We are originally constituted in such a way as to be human in this way. This is clearly brought to self-awareness in conscience, through which human beings live by being allowed to live and which involves the dictum "Heaven knows and the earth also knows." When knowledge arises in our relations with others through a self-awareness about which it is said that "Heaven knows," *shiriau* comes into being. This Japanese word is equivalent to the English phrase "to be acquainted with each other." The word "acquaintance" has the meaning of "to have intimate knowledge of." That we are said to have an intimate knowledge of others cannot be conceived of apart from this basic self-awareness. Therefore, in self-awareness there is united into one the self's concerns with other things and with other persons. And it is here that "to know oneself" comes to be established. Apart from this, self-awareness could turn out to be a self-centered consciousness in which our small self, while still conscious of itself as "I," proceeds to respond to others, and then relates itself to them. In most cases, these self-conscious concerns have the character of "evil passions," to use a term peculiar to Buddhism. They are repeated in such a way that they flow and arise, appear on the scene and then disappear, and so forth, whereby people are pleased by and grieve over matters of little or no importance. While being captives to this process of "flowing and arising," people continue to go on flowing, all together. In spite of this, I feel that ego-centeredness always prevails here. In the final analysis, it is accompanied by an air of loneliness and alienation.

But authentic solitude exists in a place in which the self is truly the self itself, a place where the fact that the self and others are to-gether—that is, "acquainted with each other"—truly arises. However contradictory it may sound, only when the dictum of "to be alone" is pushed to its logical conclusion is the relation of one individual with another truly established. When this state of affairs comes into being, a self-awareness arises in which things as well as persons are involved. Here is to be found the relation of self with something that opens up the universe and renders the self capable of being itself. I think it possible to say that this disclosure of the universe is in fact a place that actually grants to us that dimension in which self-awareness occurs. It is, after all, in the great disclosure of the universe that a self-awareness arises in which other persons, things, and the self are involved all together. Self-awareness always has this characteristic of disclosure. In making a similar point, Buddhism uses the term "mind." I think that Buddhism tries to situate the mind at a place that is inclusive of the whole. Hence, self-awareness consists in knowing one's mind. With respect to the term "mind," there is no doubt that it refers to the mind of our self. But this is not the whole story. It cannot be covered by being identified with the mere mind of our self, as it is understood in its ordinary sense. In Buddhism, there are a variety of expressions for consciousness, such as a *manōvijñānā* or *ālayavijñānā* (store-consciousness). The mind we are talking about is a mind of this sort. In the final analysis, we should say that the authentic mind is a place where things make their appearance, and where the self's relation with things, as well as with other human beings, comes to be established.

So far as the basis of this mind is concerned, I think it is possible to describe it in terms of "disclosure," which renders all the things that are called "heaven and earth" capable of being. It is quite right to use the term "power," in order to come to grips with it.

The Buddhist Concept of "True Suchness"

The term 'power' is well known in the West as well as in Buddhism. Today, the concept of power surfaces as being of great concern in both the natural and social sciences. Mention has already been made of conscience. While the "mind" as ordinarily used in Buddhism is manifested most typically in the form of Buddha-mind, the Buddha or the bodhisattvas stand out as problems to be faced with respect to power. This power appears in the Pure Land sect of Buddhism under the guise of the saving power of Amida Buddha's vow. Viewed from another angle, the original vow of Amida Buddha is understood to be power or the power of virtue. But at bottom, it is quite different from what we usually call power. Rather, we should say that what we are dealing with here is the negation of power.

What expresses this most precisely are words such as nothingness, emptiness, or *nihilum*, which constitute the fundamental basis of Buddhism. It seems to me that these words are meant to refer to something which is absolutely deprived of what we usually call authority or power such as the force of arms by which students employ power by wearing helmets. In comparison with substantial power, we might better describe what is at issue with a phrase such as "hollowed power," even though, I am afraid, there may not be such a term or phrase available in Japanese. The term "hollowed" means that there is actually no substantial power involved, and that powers, whatever they may be, disappear altogether. And what is more, if they were hollowed, they would be completely beyond our touch. With something like this in mind, Buddhism tries to come to grips with this truth by means of mind. In compliance with this view, Buddhism also speaks of a self-awareness in which we are truly said to be ourselves—that is, to be unrestrictedly free and to be able to acquire knowledge by ourselves. Everything is embedded in a term such as *tathatā* (suchness), which is peculiar to Buddhism, in place of "self-awareness." At any rate, no matter what terms you may use here—suchness, *tathatā*, or self-awareness—all have the meaning of "to know." That is, suddenly we become aware of the basis of ourselves. Since "to become aware of," in this case, arises out of its own intrinsic nature, then it is all right here for us to use the term "nature."

I made mention of power, having in mind a power that creates something novel at this very place. In my opinion, the power to create something novel is not what can be described in terms of substantial power. Rather, it possesses a quality that basically negates substantial power but at the same time possesses another aspect that allows it to activate substantial power while at the same time negating it. The most important fact to be noted here is that this apparently contradictory statement gives expression to something involving human beings and other things, which is out of the reach of power and which power is completely unable to touch. For the purpose of giving expression to this something, various negating words are used, such as hollowness, emptiness, or nothingness. I am sure that this constitutes the most basic element in Buddhism, which is described in terms of an attempt "to empty oneself," or of a hollowed mind, or of no-mindedness. I am convinced that a hollowed mind is demanded as being of importance in human friendship. The standpoint of an emptied mind is a standpoint in which we truly become ourselves. This is precisely what is meant by the term "no-mindedness." The power emerging from it has nothing to do with what we call substantial or authoritative power or the power of armed force. It is something quite different from this.

Various concepts are involved in the term "power." The power inherent in the saving power of Amida Buddha's vow is the diametrical opposite of what is ordinarily understood as power. I think it is necessary to conceive of how it works, and of the meaning of the sense of power inherent in its working. I also think that it is necessary to understand clearly what the power is that is involved in the great compassion. As I said before, the self-awareness in which we know ourselves is the same as the fact that we exist, that is, as the being of our self. The mere fact that we exist as human beings involves problems to be resolved. A human being possesses a structure that demands that he or she exists with an obligation to achieve his or her true humanity. What is more, in order for a human being to become a human being, it must be that one has something to achieve out of one's own power. Here are counted, among other things, acts, deeds, and one's path. "To go along a path" is not the same as merely to go on a walk, but is tied up with religious "practice," "discipline," or, if I extend my argument to Buddhism as a whole, with "testimony." In this way, testimony bears witness to the fact that a human being is a human being. Above, I remarked that testimony bears witness to being, that is, to the self realizing or achieving itself. In the case of the carpenter, since the house that he built is also himself, he asks other people to look at it, because it is just "I myself." After all, a state of affairs such as this has the characteristic feature of testimony in which the self exhibits itself. Therefore, one insists that one is there by saying, "I am." This does not mean that one exists in complete isolation. Instead, one is there, and if one is a carpenter, then the house is also there, which, by being related to others and by making a promise to relate to others, brings this promise to fruition. This implies the achieving of meaningful human relationships with others. We can say that one exists here as such a person, and in such a fashion. Earlier, in order to refer to this way of being human, I mentioned self-awareness. This self-awareness consists in coming "to know," and "to know" has the same meaning as "to be." So far as self-awareness is concerned, there is no difference between being and knowledge.

The Meaning of "Con" in the Term "Conscience"

In brief, conscience has both the sense of "totality" and that of "knowledge." This "totality" is denoted by the prefix "con" in English and *ge* in German. Thus in German a mountain is denoted by means of the term *Berg*, but a group of mountains is denoted by the term *Gebirge*. The prefix "con" has the same meaning. The German term *wissen* is equivalent to "to know." And "to know the totality" is equivalent to *gewissen*. Needless to say, the German term *Gewissen* is equivalent to "conscience" in English. This knowledge of totality implies self-awareness. Then what is it that takes part in the totality? Included is the "I am" in the sense mentioned above, as well as something that allows it to be or to live—that is, God or Buddha. Since God or Buddha is what allows other beings to be, God or Buddha stand on a different level than other beings. It is acceptable to say that the prefix "con" denotes the place in which those two, while being separated from each other through an infinite and absolute distance, nonetheless are unified into one as inseparable. For human beings, this state of affairs, as indicated by means of "con," is always everywhere opened up underfoot. While it is infinitely distanced from us, there is nothing nearer to us than it.

Augustine is a well-known Christian thinker. While saying that God lives within him and therefore that he lives a God-oriented life, he insists that in his life he is more obedient to God than he is to himself. We are inclined to think that it is with ourselves that we are most familiar. This is a standpoint in which a self-centered consciousness is predominant. But speaking more fundamentally on the ground that

God is the Creator of us human beings, he is to be found at the deepest depths of our existence. Because of his being the source through which we are created, it is said that God is by far nearer to us than we are to ourselves. Viewed from another angle, God and a human being—that is, the Creator and the created—cannot be taken together. They are absolutely far away from each other. But at the same time, they are near to each other to the extent that God is nearer to the human self than it is to itself. These two things must be simultaneously spoken of here.

At the bottom of conscience understood in this sense lurks the fact that "Heaven knows and the earth also knows." That we know ourselves means that we are known by God or by Buddha. I would like to ask your patience in repeating my conviction that "to know" in the sense of our knowing God or Buddha has nothing to do with the knowledge by which we know things objectively, while presupposing their existence as over there. "To know" in this fundamental sense is united with the fact that we exist. For this reason, one will surely be prevented from understanding the matter under consideration if one supposes that one's existence is here, and that God exists over there, and then one comes to know him objectively. Rather, the fact is that the two things—both the self's existence and knowledge—are established at one and at the same time. For this reason, once the self truly comes to know itself, it is not that it becomes conscious of itself ambiguously, but rather that it becomes awakened to its real features, saying, "This is 'I.' " This self-awareness in Buddhism takes various forms, depending on differences such as the gate of the Holy Path or that of the Pure Land. In spite of this, there is no difference with respect to the fact that we come to know ourselves in such a fashion that we become aware of, and are awakened to, ourselves in one way or another. This is the reason why I said before that knowledge of this sort is connected to the Absolute. We all take part in knowledge of this sort, which is quite different from objective and discursive knowledge.

The world is spoken of in various ways. To use a term that is characteristic of Buddhism, we might think of it in the form of "three thousand worlds." Nowadays, in place of this, we speak of a universe in which individual things, inclusive of human beings, appear in their own individual forms. Most representative of this universe is the world of nature, in which mountains and rivers, grasses and plants, and so forth exist. Roughly speaking, we can divide the world into three: the world of things; that of human beings; and that of what has been called the Absolute, that is, God or Buddha.

Conscience consists in the self-knowledge that the self knows itself. Here the term "self" indicates that each human being knows himself or herself as such. The "self," which is manifest in the fact that the self knows by itself whether or not the water is cold or warm, is established at one and the same time as the fact that in the "self," knowledge is also involved. If these two are separated, then we have no alternative but to suppose that the self exists somewhere objectively, and to look at it from the outside in an objective manner. This latter view consists in knowing something as an object, in the sense of a subject-object dichotomy. If so, then the self cannot truly be conceived, nor can the fact that the self exists. Let us take account of the fact that the self is said to know itself. If the self is presupposed from the outset and comes to know itself as something that is looked at from outside of itself, as if the known self were something different from the knowing one, then what is predominant is a standpoint of consciousness that prevents the genuine sense of being and of knowledge from coming to the fore. This is the standpoint of objective knowledge—that is, of discriminative knowledge based on the dichotomy of subject and object.

The self truly exists. This existence appears simultaneously in the form of self-awareness. Here a human being is regarded as a self-awaked being, or as the self-awareness of being. "To be" and "to know" are meant to be taken as one and the same. When standing on this position of self-awareness, I think it possible to conceive of the self as embodying dharma, to use a Buddhist term that is inclusive of the whole, and in which other human beings, society, the world of nature, and God or Buddha are all involved. In dharma are brought to unification the Buddha himself and all of the things in the world. Therefore, knowledge is nothing other than knowledge of dharma. When it is said that the knowledge of dharma and that of the self come to arise as one, the structure of this self will remain unknown if we think of it as ego-centered, and try to extend the objective knowing activity to God or Buddha on the basis of this ego. It would be better to think of an empty-minded standpoint as the most basic one. In this emptied mind, we are out of ourselves and into the world in which we relate to other persons and things from the beginning. We stand here in the disclosure in which God or Buddha is revealed. Fundamentally speaking, this knowledge is different from ordinary knowledge. It is only in this sense that the dharma of Buddha is truly understood.

Conscience Makes Its Appearance in the West

Before Gotama Buddha died, he told his followers not to rely on him, but admonished them rather to rely on the dharma, to hold up the dharma as a light, and to make themselves a light as well. This means to look for a guiding star in dharma. This admonition of Gotama is based on a method through which we try to become ourselves through and through.

I am confident that conscience is very much like this. I think it quite important to inquire as to how conscience is expressed in Buddhism. Indeed, conscience arises as an issue in the present age in a variety of ways. If we try to deal with this issue in the full sense described above, then conscience seems to make its appearance everywhere. For instance, for those students who try to appeal to armed force for the purpose of realizing their cause, there is a problem in that they fail to obey the true dictates of their conscience, while trying to be conscientious.

The same sort of thing appears at various places in the history of the Western world. Viewed from a philosophical standpoint, it is in Socrates that the issue of conscience is brought out in the most conspicuous relief. His dictum "Know thyself" is well known. To begin with, this dictum admonishes other people to know their own ignorance. Over against those who pretend to know about ultimate things— namely, the intelligentsia of those days, such as the Sophists, people with a vast stock of information at hand, and men of culture—he leveled his criticism by saying that the knowledge possessed by these so-called intelligent people is not authentic knowledge. We gain access to his way of thinking primarily through Plato's writings, and according to Plato, Socrates went to the Sophists and held dialogues with them. His method was to start from the premise or the assumption that he did not know anything, to then hear intelligent people voice various opinions, to raise questions about what they said, and finally to lead them to a state in which they are at a loss as to what answer is appropriate, or to a conclusion that is incompatible with what they said in the beginning. This is the method of question and answer.

As a consequence, his dictum "Know thyself" is meant to admonish us to truly know ourselves instead of having a stock of opinions. At bottom is that knowledge which is acquired by one's self. I think that this is an important implication of conscience. Viewed from this vantage point, an intelligent person of ordinary caliber is not conscientious. Contented with oneself, one does not know that one still falls short of something vital, and that one is ignorant. But Socrates, however ignorant he may have been, at least knew that he was ignorant. In this respect, he was conscientious, and took a truly conscientious standpoint—that is, the standpoint from which the self knows itself in a far wider sense than what is ordinarily thought to be morally conscientious.

Socrates received from the famous Delphic oracle the claim that he was the wisest person. But why is he who is ignorant called the wisest person? This was a divine message. What does this divine message mean? Pondering these things, he was led to the conclusion that, even though he is ignorant, at least he knows that he is ignorant. In spite of the fact that they think they know everything, other intellectuals do not really know their own ignorance, and hence they do not truly know themselves. Socrates, who is ignorant, knows that he is so. In this respect, he is one step ahead of them. The place from which he is ahead of them is connected with the divine message. Here, at bottom, lies a fundamental characteristic of conscience.

Thus, conscience takes its departure from the dictum "Know thyself." What Socrates wanted to do by engaging in discussion was to make clear that it is one's duty to pursue a true grasp of things by raising such questions as, for example, what courage is , what justice is, and so forth. This procedure does not involve him alone. Instead, his method is to start from the stage at which he does not know anything, and to proceed thence to argue various issues with others, using his method of question and answer. In this way, those who pretend to be intellectual are forced to become aware of their ignorance. Socrates then says that if we are all ignorant about ourselves, we should study together. Thus, the starting line for the acquisition of authentic wisdom is first drawn here. This starting line is drawn for the purpose of establishing community between one person and another, for they, while raising questions and giving answers, rely on the same *logos* and try to reach mutual agreement on the ground that this *logos* gives assurance that they can finally come to agree on opinions.

There human beings can truly rely on each other. Socrates takes the standpoint of reason, which is equivalent in meaning to intellect or *logos*. Since they all participate in the same reason, human beings can come to agree on matters of opinion and ways of thinking. And what is more, through this participation truth is disclosed, which consists of the same *logos*, at least so far as its content is concerned. When all of their minds come together in such a way as to terminate in the giving birth to a sense of the reasonableness of things, then *logos* makes its appearance under the guise of the reasonableness of truth. I think that this is the standpoint of reason. And I am convinced that at the bottom of reason lurks conscience, which tells us to honestly confess that we do not know what we do not know, and that we do not, in the final analysis, know anything about even what we think we have come to know. In brief, conscience tells us to know ourselves. I think that this statement is made on the basis of having walked along the path toward conscience, understood in the sense that we continue to explore our authentic self.

Conscience is Concerned with One's Making Sure of Oneself

After Socrates, Plato and Aristotle followed suit, and thus a great tradition of thinking called "Greek philosophy" developed. Within the development of this way of thinking, as is evident in Socrates, they came back to God as a natural consequence. The term "God," in this context, is meant to refer to reason, for at the bottom of reason lurks God. Plato and Aristotle carry on their philosophy by keeping an eye on this issue.

If we take into consideration the man called Jesus in Christianity, I am sure that the issue of conscience is also manifest somewhere in his teaching. For instance, when he preached the Gospels for the first time, it is reported that he said, "The Kingdom of God is near; repent." The term "repent" is equivalent to "conversion"—that is to say, to turn around the direction of mind. This is repentance. The basic meaning of it consists in changing the direction of one's mind, namely, in substituting a new mind for the old one. And it is said that in connection with this, the Kingdom of God is approaching. What is now before us is something quite historical and temporal. That the absolute Kingdom of God is coming near means that disclosure is coming forth out of the minds of human beings. Recently, much use has been made of the term "eschatological." I get the impression that Jesus's dictum "The Kingdom of God is approaching; repent" has an eschatological implication. In my opinion, what is now under consideration is, after all, in its structure quite similar to conscience, for through this dictum Jesus admonishes each of us to return to his or her genuine self. At that time, the religious body of Judaism was quite in favor of the establishment, and was represented by law-abiding Pharisees. Ordered to do this or that in their social life, and thus deprived of their vigor for life, people were forced to be buried beneath these prescriptions. They were obliged to observe various laws and rules, many of which were difficult to keep, including the Sabbath. For this reason, Jesus said that human beings do not exist for the Sabbath. In this way, the consciousness that the Sabbath exists for human beings returns to human beings. At the bottom of the fact that a human being returns to being vigorously human lies Jesus's admonition of repentance. It aims to turn a human being, who is buried under various restrictions, in the direction of conscience. At the rear of the emergence of this new direction lurks the fact that the Kingdom of God is approaching. At the place where the arrival of this kingdom is susceptible of being felt bodily, human beings are admonished to repent—that is, to transform the direction of their minds. This insight lies at the basis of Christianity.

Jesus's admonition is concerned not only with knowledge, as is the case with Socrates, but also with a human being as a whole. It goes without saying that Socrates made many efforts to impart something novel to his society and to his country, just as Jesus did with his, and both imparted something novel to human relationships. Even though both of them turned their attention to God, they tried to substitute a new god for the old-fashioned one.

Socrates brought about a reformation in thinking. In this attempt as well, there lurked his intention to reform his country—that is, to bring about a social reformation, to use contemporary terminology. But what he wanted to achieve took its departure from the basic re-forming of a human being. This is an important point to keep in mind. The structure is the same with Jesus. He said that we cannot repent unless we change completely. For this purpose, God was conceived from another angle and, as a result, the new disclosure of God was accounted for in connection with the reformation of a human being. In this regard, there is no difference between Socrates and Jesus.

I think that this is also the case with Augustine. For instance, in his autobiography, the well-known word "confession" is used. Apart from the standpoint of conscience, there can be no confession. What he wants to assert by means of this word is the confessing of one's sins, but this is quite different from confessing crimes that one has committed, when being arrested by the police. "Sin" has to do with that for which no one in society is to blame, but concerning which one's conscience cannot rest satisfied. At the same time, one should speak of sin as based on that circumstance which one has in mind, and about which one is ashamed, but which one cannot afford to disclose to the public. It has to do with a certain reproach of one's own conscience. To disclose this before God—this is confession. Of course, in Catholicism during the Middle Ages confession regularly took place secretly before a monk. A monk is a representative of God, and people confess before God what they cannot allow as a public disclosure.

The most basic feature of conscience lies in a certain unsettledness concerning which one cannot truly be oneself, if something continues to be left undone. This is exactly what I said before in terms of the reproach of conscience. In this case, one is lured into giving expression to it in any way possible. A carpenter is under pressure to express himself through his work in building a house and not leaving something undone. He tries to do this through his dealing with wood and through his bodily activities. In the case of confession, expression is given on the outside in the form of communicating "through language." The phrase "on the outside" is meant to refer to being "before God," which is far more fundamental than being before the public. Here the activity of conscience permeates the whole. Roughly speaking, the standpoint of conscience consists in one's feeling unsatisfied with oneself, and hence feeling the pricks of conscience.

The prefix "con" in the term "confession" has the same meaning as the prefix "con" in conscience. It means that one acknowledges oneself and discloses this acknowledgment in such a way as to put something hidden before the public. To put something hidden before the public, by saying "This is it," means that one opens oneself to others. That is to say, for someone to open up in this way is to recognize one's own sin. One opens oneself up so as to inform others of who one is oneself. In this way, confession consists in disclosing oneself to others with the help of language.

This is, after all, a result of the activity of conscience. In addition, a third person is also involved here, and a matter of fact is clearly brought to light. But although human relationships come to intervene here, the dictum that indicates that one stands "before God" is the most basic. And it is conscience that permeates this structure as a whole. Here the term "conscience" should be taken in the sense of holistic knowledge or of self-awareness, as dealt with earlier. What Augustine tries to convey in terms of confession has, fundamentally speaking, precisely this quality. In confession, one tries to be truthful to oneself through and through. At the same time, one is here before one's God. This is the self-knowledge in which "Heaven knows and the earth also knows" occurs, and in which one tries to be faithful to one's God. This is the standpoint of Christianity.

One more thing is to be noted here. Descartes speaks of conscience, which is to be regarded as knowledge. He set out to doubt all things, including God, as well as the supposed fact that there is something in the world. Nothing is certain. Therefore, he is in search of certainty or assurance. The issue of certainty is to be considered together with the possibility of truthfulness. Strictly speaking, many things are involved here. But the point for us is to be sure about ourselves, or to look for the certainty within ourselves. Taking up the position of self-consciousness, people used to say that they wanted to be sure of themselves. With this in view, they dared to challenge authority by holding clubs of *Gewalt*, ("steel clubs," power). In such a way, they expressed a desire to confirm themselves. Their standpoint is ordinarily characterized in terms of belligerent atheism. But I am sure that what drove them to it was their desire to be sure of themselves. It seems to me that the issue of conscience involves a motive similar to that. But the fundamental difference has to do with the place in which to look for certainty. In the case of aggressive atheism, everything is carried on with the ego as its center.

In Marxism, the motive for various things such as social justice, the state, its authority, or its established order may come into question. But the present state of Marxism deviates to a great extent from the standpoint in which all these things are fundamentally connected. These things are held in separation from each other, and fail to be unified. Or rather, here all things revolve around the standpoint of ego, and come together at this point. The standpoint of the whole, as is characterized by the prefix "con" or *ge*, here fails to be brought out in bold relief. I am sure that atheism of this sort stops short of the most basic thing—that is, a somewhat all-encompassing standpoint with which religions have been concerned since ancient times. Even though subjectivity is here spoken of, it falls victim to a quite self-centered standpoint. And even if social justice is demanded, this standpoint is eager to discriminate between friend and foe, and does not abhor the assassination of others. Descartes, while taking up the standpoint of knowledge as philosophy, set out a method of finding certainty by subjecting all things to doubt, and finally came back to his self-doubting by affirming that this doubting self could by no means be doubted. "Cogito ergo sum." This is, after all, the standpoint of conscience, which is quite similar to Socrates' view. While subjecting all things to doubt by saying that there is nothing truly reliable because everything is uncertain, he was finally led to the conclusion that the fact that he is now doubting cannot be doubted at all, and, hence, that there is the self now doubting. Here the ego makes its appearance. Descartes took his start from this and went from there to the existence of God, and even further to the existence of the world. After coming to know the existence of God and the world of nature, he came back again to himself as the final stage. But in his case, we must also say that the standpoint of religion, in which we live while being allowed to live, does not come to the fore. Of course, this criticism is raised against him by taking the side of Christianity, in which the creation of God is assured. But looking at his view from the standpoint of the present, we must say that a major problem is left unresolved. However this may be, while coming to know himself through the method of doubt, he reached the certainty that he exists, and on the basis of this he tried to deal with God, the world, and other human beings. In this structure of thought conscience is involved.

Nihilism and Religion

Whenever a fresh start is made in the history of Western philosophy, Socrates, Augustine, and Descartes are called forth. Socrates is the source of philosophy in ancient times, Augustine in the Middle Ages, and Descartes in the modern age. This means that whenever something novel occurs in philosophy, a fresh start is made by going back to the self. I think that it is here that conscience comes to the fore. Marxism also came into question in the above. I think it very important to give due consideration to such issues.

The basic problem that Buddhism now confronts focuses on this very point. In my lecture, I had wanted to refer to various Buddhist sūtras, but to my regret, I have been unable to do that to my satisfaction. In an attempt to deal with how Buddhism thinks of conscience, it seems to be inevitable to conceive of the problem in terms of what the issue of conscience is like in the contemporary world, or of what it means for a Buddhist to be conscientious. I think that various difficulties arise here—for example, problems such as a very active religious organization, the present situation of Buddhism, and so forth. But more fundamentally, there is now another very difficult problem pressing on Buddhism, just as it is on Christianity. The issue Christianity is now facing is atheism.

Marxism surfaces as a belligerent atheism. Behind the logic of those students who have recourse to the force of arms lurks a belligerent atheism. It appears as a refusal to accept a religious standpoint from the outset. It is a well-known fact that Marxism originated in atheism.

One more thing to be noted here is that an atheism of this sort, when pushed to its logical consequence, is a form of nihilism whose catchphrase is "God is dead." At present, Christianity in particular is confronted by this issue. In my opinion, the foremost problem with which Christianity must cope right now is the issue of God's existence. Of course, it is out of the question to deal with this issue in a way that completely deviates from the traditional God of Christianity. But what is now demanded of Christianity is that it deal with it in an entirely new way that is different from the traditional understanding, but at the same time includes it. I think that in order to meet this demand, there is no alternative but to deal with, and to confront,

Marxism, atheism, and the nihilism inherent in the present natural and social sciences.

I think that in the case of Buddhism, the same difficulty appears on the scene. For instance, since the Shin sect of Buddhism is based on the decline of Buddhist Law in latter days, dharma is not here regarded in its correct form; its deterioration is already under way. It is a matter of fact that this sect of Buddhism is established on the basis of such an understanding. But, at present, there is one further question as to exactly how we are able to understand the Buddha and the Pure Land. Whereas the Buddha and the Pure Land cannot be separated from each other, this matter is a pressing one for Buddhism as an issue to be tackled through its confrontation with atheistic nihilism, as it appears in the West, and in Christianity in particular, since atheistic nihilism is now an issue for Buddhism as well.

There is a chapter entitled *"Jorōbon"* (Buddha's Span of Life") in the *Lotus Sūtra*, in which the death of Gotama Buddha is questioned. But he is infinite in life and is permanent. His dying right now cannot be conceived of, since he is the eternally enlightened Buddha who entered into nirvāna countless aeons ago. Behind the problem concerning the fact that the Buddha died, questions need to be raised, it seems to me, as to why the Buddha, who had already entered into nirvāna, should die, and what in the world the death of Buddha is supposed to mean. These questions are related to the fact that Gotama Buddha really did die. As a consequence, the parable of the famous good physician is cited in this sūtra. It goes as follows: Once upon a time, there was an expert in medicine. He took a long journey. He had several children who had been writhing in agony, for they had taken poison while he was absent. Among them were some children whose minds were kept sound, and others who had gone mad because the poison had passed into their whole bodies. When the father had them take medicine, the former group recovered, but the latter refused all medicines. This is the story. It is a simile concerning Buddha and other sentient beings. The father is regarded as Buddha, and the children represent sentient beings. Buddha tries to give dharma to sentient beings suffering from disease, but among them, there are some who rebel against it.

The story continues. Pondering this matter, the clever physician set out on the journey once again, saying, "Since I am old, I may soon die. I will leave these medicines here. Take them even after I am dead." Then from his resting place on the journey, he sent a messenger to inform them of his death. They felt alone and lamented their solitude on the ground that their father had passed away. He could have rescued them from their illness, had he been alive. But this grief gradually helped them to recover consciousness, and they were finally cured as a result of having taken the medicines.

The moral of this parable is that the eternally enlightened Buddha died, in spite of the impossibility of his dying since he was enlightened, and that because there is too much emphasis upon his permanent achievement of nirvāna, his followers fell into idle habits that hindered them from paying homage to him. This parable also tells us that Buddha died for the purpose of letting his followers know how compassionate Buddha is, and how difficult it is to encounter him and of alluring them into having the desire to pay homage to him. Therefore, the contention that Buddha died is not a true fact, but an instance of skill of means. Emphasis is here placed on the view that even though it is skill of means, it is not a lie. The crux of the story rests on the view that Buddha died for the purpose of letting people truly come to know him.

What is now under debate in Christianity is somewhat similar to this parable, which tells us that Buddha leaves the earth and disappears, but remains active. Behind this story is the fact that the Buddha is an eternally enlightened one, and that his death is only a temporary expedient. Basically speaking, this might be what the story tries to tell us. But the important thing for us is to submit the moral of this story to serious reconsideration in the context of the present situation. For instance, it is necessary to put issues such as Buddha's death and the meaning of nirvāna into the context of our present situation, and to ponder the implications of these matters. After all, such issues are entangled with questions about atheism and nihilism. I think that something similar happens with respect to the various issues concerning the world and human beings.

At any rate, the fact is that we cannot yet stand on conscience, that is, on that on which we feel ourselves settled and truly assured. I think it absolutely necessary to be in search of clarification of such issues constantly. Through our endeavor to assess what role conscience plays in present-day Buddhism, we must come to grips anew with the Buddha and with the basic standpoint of Buddhism. It is true, however, that our endeavor will be of no use if it disregards the traditional way of thinking that is characteristic of Buddhism. I think that the same can be said for Christianity.

GLOSSARY OF JAPANESE TERMS

anshinritsumei.   our mind becomes settled and our life is finally established

basho.   place, as in the Greek *topos*. It is that base out of which the subject-object separation arises.

bukkokudo.   the Buddha Realm

dōbō.   fellow human beings

en.   (karmic) ties, destiny

fueki.   the state of no change

fuekiryukō.   *fueki* means "no change," "the eternal," and *ryukō* means "change," "transformation," or "fashionableness." One changes, and yet returns to ones eternal roots.

fugichi.   knowledge beyond doubt

ho.   brothers and sisters

hō.   dharma, that is, Buddhist truth as expounded by Gotama Buddha

hōben.   a skillful means to an end, a temporary expedient *ikikata.* a way of living one's life

inochi. living one's life as ordered from above

izukatae. whereto?

ji. the viewpoint of actuality

jinen. an adverb meaning "of itself," "spontaneously," or "naturally." Shinran (1173–1263) used *jinen* to refer to formless true reality, emptiness, suchness, thusness, oneness. To be brought to awakening throught he Buddha's teaching is *jinen*. Thus, *jinen* is itself the Pure Land, achieved naturally, spontaneously, and not through one's own planning and calculation.

jiriki. self-power: in Zen Buddhist teaching, spiritual progress is achieved by one's own efforts, one's own power.

jitafuni. self and others are not two, the self and others cannot be separated from one another

jōdo. the Pure Land

kata. form

kihō. the mind of a sentient being believing in the Buddha's power to bring one to realization

kōshikondō. to mix up public and private matters

koto. a work

kyōgaibetsuden. this is a way of thinking to which Zen Buddhism has resorted in explicating salvation through self-power. According to this way of thinking, Buddhist truth is transmitted directly by the Buddha even beyond the various Buddhist teachings and sūtras.

makoto. truthfulness, trustworthiness

misoshiru.	miso soup
monpō.	to listen to Buddha's teachings
nembutsu.	prayers to Buddha
ningen.	human being, person
nori.	a law; starting to talk
ōyake.	public
reidanjichi.	by one's own bodily experiences one must come to know whether water is cool or warm
ri.	reason; a pattern of ideal human relationships
rihō.	the rational law
rin.	fellows; a system of relations
rinri.	ethics; the order or pattern through which the communal existence of human beings is made possible
ryōchi.	good knowledge
ryōnō.	great intellect, an innate gift of great intelligence
ryōshin.	conscience
ryukō.	fashionable; undergoing constant change
shin.	mind
shiriau.	to be acquainted, to have intimate knowledge of another
shōjōshu.	the stage at which a believer is assured of becoming a Buddha

shōzōmatsu.   the tripartite scheme of the Buddhist theory of history, that is, the true dharma, the semblance dharma, and the decayed dharma

sumanai.   things are left unfinished

tariki.   other-power; contrasts with *jiriki*, or self-power. Self-power theorists believe that the way to enlightenment is through our own efforts, our own work. Other-power proponents believe that enlightenment (or salvation) is a gift from Buddha, a reaching down of the divine to offer us grace, and is not the result of our efforts alone.

tomodachi.   a friend

tsukemono.   a kind of pickle

watakushi.   privacy

yū.   a standpoint in which knowledge and deed are united into one

INDEX

Absolute, the, 11, 20 (note 8), 60, 146;
  as "authentic," 93;
  relation/ship to, 15–16, 92, 136;
  as unchangeable, 58, 73, 135;
  we encounter, 13
Adam, and Eve, 8;
  fall, 41;
  purge from the Garden of Eden, 40
ālayavijnānā (store-consciousness; a term employed by the Yogācāra School of Buddhism), 142. See also *mānovijnānā*
alienation, 10, 85;
  and ego-centeredness, 142;
  from a loss of trustworthiness, 82;
  and natural sciences, 97–98;
  preventing authentic human relationships, 80
allowed to be/live, 6, 14, 123–26, 128, 129, 130, 135, 136, 141, 145, 153. *See also* other-power; *tariki*
Amida/Amida Buddha, 6, 7, 11, 87, 106;
  saving power of, 143, 144
Amitabha (the Buddha of infinite light), 7
anarchism, 133
anshinritsumei (life becomes settled), 129
Aristotle, 89, 150
artisan spirit, the, 94–95

Association of the Great Earth (Shin Buddhist), 1, 20 (note 1), 65, 71
atheism, 155, 156;
  belligerent, 129, 153–54
attitude, as a way of living or direction, 24–25, 26, 31, 42;
  of "knowing things as they really are," 99;
  transformation of, 47
Augenblick (now, here, instant, the moment), 49
Augustine, 53, 145, 151, 152, 154
authentic contact, between clergy and laity, 33–34
authentic falsity, 120
authenticity, 3, 10, 17–18, 55, 115
authentic life, 129. See also *makoto*
authentic person, 3
authentic (human) relationship/s, 1–2;
  trustworthiness makes possible, 10;
  prevention of, 80
authentic self, 19, 139, 150

Barth, Karl, and conscience, 53;
  dialectical theology, 73;
  and world Christianity, 64
basho (place, field , matrix), 9, 10, 15
being, and time, 48–49;
  cannot be separated from place, 83–84;
  of a human being, 80–81, 84–85, 144;
  and nothingness, 48, 80

Being and Time, Heidegger's, 48
Berg (mountain), 145
Beruf (to call), 128
betweenness, 9, 10, 13, 16, 83. See also *basho*
Bible, 23, 24, 25, 26, 29
bird's-eye view, 59–60, 61
Blut und Boden (blood and soil), 13–14, 123
bō (brothers and sisters), 83. See also *dōbō*
bodhisattva/s, 13, 66–67, 68, 84, 106, 143;
  sprang from the ground, 66–68
Bragt, Jan Van, ix, 2, 20 (note 2)
Buber, Martin, 10, 11, 92–93, 96. See also "I and thou"
Buddha, allows beings to be, 145;
  and Buddha-nature, 2, 16;
  and compassion, 99;
  and saving power, 143;
  as Miroku, 106–7;
  as ultimate cause, 101, 106;
  death of, 147, 155–56;
  dharma and *sangha*, 48–49, 52;
  knowledge of, 99;
  land of the, 14, 66, 84, 86, 88, 123, 125;
  law of, 121;
  light of, 99;
  manifestations of, 65;
  teachings of, 45
Buddhahood, 2
Buddha-mind, 16–17, 113–14, 143. See also Buddha-nature
Buddha-nature, 2, 6, 9, 10, 11, 16–17;
  all sentient beings possess, 86–88;
  is Tathāgata, 88. See also Tathāgata;
  and *ryōshin*, 113;
  something unchangeable, 10–11, 86–87
Buddhism, aloofness from this world, 15, 16, 112–13;
  attempt to reappropriate, 32;
  and bodhisattvas, 143;

and Confucianism, 51;
and conscience, 15–16, 53, 148, 154;
and certainty, 55;
and compassion, 6–7, 99, 144, 156;
and dogma, 25–26;
and emptiness, viii, 8, 38, 143–44. *See also* emptiness; nothingness;
and enlightenment, 58, 104;
and ethics, 8, 38, 51–52;
and evil passions, 142;
and foolishness, 105;
and faith, 56, 72, 76;
and the general public, 47;
and historical consciousness, 39–40, 45, 49, 52, 58–59, 63;
and interdependent origination, 13, 101;
and knowledge, 104, 146–47;
and living one's own life, 34;
and the Middle Path, 80;
and mind, 142–44;
and modernization, 2, 5, 36–38, 44, 63, 69, 71–72, 88;
and the modern world, 9, 63–64;
and suffering, 9, 49–50;
and suchness, 143;
and ties (*en*), 78;
and Western culture, 2–3;
as bird's-eye view, 60;
as unchanged, 31;
as an emergent field, 9, 50;
four great agents of, 65–66. *See also* great elements;
gap of opinion in, 23. *See also* gap;
human body in, the, 81, 83;
influence on Wang Yang-Ming, 112;
Land of the Buddhas, ix, 6, 66, 84, 86, 88, 106–7. *See also* Kingdom of God; Pure Land, the;
Mahāyāna, 59, 80;
nihilum (nothingness, emptiness) as the basis of, 143. *See also* emptiness; nothingness;

nonduality of oneself and other,
79–80, 93;
"skill of means," 118–20. See also
hōben;
three learnings of (precepts,
enlightenment, wisdom), 50;
three pillars/treasures of (Buddha,
dharma, sangha), 48–50, 52;
true Law, semblance Law, and
the declining Law, the, 121;
See also interdependent origination; Pure Land Buddhism
Buddhist ethics, the ground of, 17
bukkokudo (Buddha Realm), viii
Bultmann, R, 73

capitalism, basis of Western, 8;
tied to Christianity, 39
Catholicism, 151
ceremony, 25, 78;
as a form of religious service, 26
certainty, 54–56, 77, 79, 86, 152–54.
See also faith; uncertainty
Ch'an Buddhism, 7. See also Zen
Buddhism
Christ, 3, 8, 40, 41;
Christianity, and atheism, 154–55;
and capitalism, 8, 39;
and conscience, 9, 59, 150–51, 156;
and Descartes, 153;
and ethics, 9, 51–52, 59;
and faith, 72, 76–77;
and Greek thought, 9, 51;
and history, 40–41, 43, 50, 59, 73;
and individuality, 92;
and Kierkegaard, 93;
and the Kingdom of God, 66–67,
84, 124, 150–51;
and truthfulness, 152;
as theology, 54;
breaking down of, 122;
characteristic features of, 25;
God in, 55;
has lost its power, 119;
in North America, 120;

openness to, ix;
and personality, 59;
primeval, 41;
problems in, 23;
relationship between God and
human beings, 63–64;
trust and God, 130;
See also Puritanism
Chu Hsi, the school of, 16;
critical attitude towards Buddhism,
112–13
Chung yung, 77
clearing, Heidegger's, 15
Climate and Culture, Watsuji's, 103
"Cogito ergo sum." See Descartes
"con" (totality, as a whole), 54, 137,
145, 152, 153
confession, 128, 151–52
Confucianism, 9, 15, 51, 77, 111–12,
127–28, 129, 130;
influence on Japanese ethics, 111–
13;
and man's faithfulness or truthfulness, 77;
Neo-, 16
Confucius, discourses of, 135
conscience, and being allowed to
live, 141;
and certainty, 153–54;
and coming back to ourselves, 60;
and conscientiousness, 140;
and ethics, 8, 9, 38, 59, 93–94,
111–13, 127, 129, 131;
and faith, 137;
and "Heaven knows." See
"Heaven knows";
and historical conscience, 8;
and human relations, 127. See also
human relations;
and religion, 3, 58–59, 130;
and shame, 94, 136, 151;
and subjectivity, 11;
and truthfulness, 129–30, 152;
and the unfinished, 11–12. See also
truthfulness;

conscience *(continued)*
  as Buddha-mind, 17–18. *See also*
    Buddha-mind;
  as enlightenment, 19, 63;
  as the good mind, 16;
  as hidden, viii–ix, 55, 94, 126, 128,
    136, 152;
  as individual, viii–ix;
  as knowledge, 19, 145;
  as knowledge acquired only by
    one's self, 57, 93–94;
  as unsettled, 53–54;
  Buddhist sense of, 18;
  carpenter analogy, 95, 126–28,
    130, 134, 138, 144–45, 151–52;
  in the West, 111, 147–48;
  is not scientific knowledge, 56–57;
  nature of, 2;
  reproaches us, 14–15, 93–94, 111,
    126–28, 130, 151–52;
  underlying reason, 149–50;
  See also confession; *ryōshin*
conscientiousness, 18, 19, 127
conscious mind, 17
consciousness, 17, 41, 103, 142, 147,
    155–56;
  and conscience, 137–39;
  of discrimination, 138–39;
  self-, 17, 137–38, 139–40, 152–53;
  vs self-awareness, 139–42
Consciousness-Only school, 52, 80
"corrupt and vile world *sive* the
    land of serene light, the," 125
"corrupt and vile world *sive* the
    Pure Land, the," 66–68
craftsman, 11, 19
creation, of the world, 40
creative power, unchangeable, 135
Cromwell, Oliver, 119

daemon, Socrates's, 12, 94–95
De Bary, Wm. Theodore, 20 (note 8)
Delphic oracle, 149
Denshūroku (collection of sayings of
    Wang Yang-ming), 112. *See also*
    Wang, Yang-ming

dependence, mutual, 141
Descartes, 152, 154;
  "Cogito ergo sum," 153;
  existence of God, 153–54
dharma (teachings, doctrine, truth,
    virtue, righteousness), 40, 47,
    51, 52, 58, 72, 155;
  admonishment to rely on, 147–48;
  self as embodying, 147;
  transcendent of time, 48–49, 50
Dilworth, David A., 20 (note 5)
disclosure, 83, 126, 143, 150;
  and conscience, 136;
  and knowledge of God or
    Buddha, 147, 151;
  and the self, 102;
  at the ground of being, 78–79;
  of mind, 84;
  of the universe, 19, 142;
  place of, 15
Divine Providence, 43, 59–60
divorce, 118–19, 122. *See also* family:
    breakdown of
dōbō (fellow human beings), 83
Dōgen (1200–1253), 23, 24, 29, 48,
    87. See also *Shōbōgenzō*
dogma, 3, 9, 26–27, 28, 54;
  dogmas, distinguishing, 25;
  of Buddhism, 50
Dostoevsky, F., 67

earth, viii, 6, 8, 9, 10, 11, 13, 14, 19,
    64–68, 98, 127–28, 130, 136, 156
economics, 34–35, 39, 43, 74, 112,
    122, 125
ego/s, 2, 19, 139, 153
ego-centered/ness, 8–9, 10–11, 15, 18,
    47–48, 64–65, 77, 79, 142, 147;
  egoistic, 140;
  ego-self, 7;
  See also alienation; God-centeredness;
    other-centeredness; self-centered
egoless, 15–16. *See also* no-self
eidos (form), 96
Einstein, 104

emptiness, viii, ix (note 2), 143–44.
    See also Buddhism: *nihilum*;
    nothingness
en (obligations, ties), 78
engagement (a relation of pledging),
    78
enlightenment, 3, 6, 7, 9, 13, 16, 17,
    18, 19, 33, 50, 57, 58–59, 63,
    104–5;
    as coming back to ourselves, 133;
    See also self-knowledge; self-
    realization
entity, 2, 89–90;
    always an individual, 91
equality, 44
Erde (earth, ground), 67
eschaton (end times), 40–41
ethics, and authenticity, 17–18;
    and Buddhism, 8–9, 15, 38–39;
    and conscience, 17, 111, 127;
    and human relationships, 1, 17,
    114–15. *See also* human rela-
    tions;
    and the land, 123–26;
    and Protestantism, 41;
    as a basic motive power, 39;
    as the basic way of living, 116–18;
    as essential, 118;
    as related to something Absolute,
    136;
    and self-knowledge, 19
existence, and anxiety, 54;
    awareness of, 62–63;
    as irreplaceability, 92;
    as place, 66;
    nature of, 52;
    reinterpretation of, 34
experimentation, 8, 44, 120

faith, and certainty, 55–56, 58, 76–77;
    and conscience, 137;
    and human existence, 72;
    and knowledge acquired by one's
    self, 57–58, 64;
    and the Pure and impure land,
    106–7;

and self-realization, 58;
    and trust, 130;
    articles of, 25–26;
    as an act of commitment, 9;
    as indubitability, 9;
    as testimony, 9;
    by faith alone, 56;
    faithfulness, 76–77;
    in Moroku, 107;
    involving something unchange-
    able, 58, 72–73;
    standpoint of, 65;
    See also conscience; *sola fide*;
    testimony
family, 24;
    authentic, 116–18;
    breakdown of, 85–86, 122–23. See
    also divorce
fatalism, 59, 126
foolishness, and true knowledge,
    105
four relations, 136, 137
freedom, 39, 61, 62, 63, 122;
    human, 44, 59, 60, 115;
    and necessity, 126
fueki (state of no change), 135
fuekiryūkō (unchangeableness and
    fashionableness), 135
function, 95–97, 100;
    social, 126–27
fugichi (knowledge beyond doubt),
    55

gap, between the public and
    religious organizations, 5, 23,
    29–31, 33–34, 47, 53, 65
Garden of Eden, 40
Gebirge (group of mountains), 145.
    See also *Berge*
Gemeinschaft (association), 85
geschehen (to come about, to befall),
    74–75, 78–79
Geschichte (a story), distinguished
    from *Historie*, 74
Gesellschaft (profit motive in
    capitalist society), 85

Gewalt (an act of violence), 152–53
Gewissen (to know, conscience), 54,
  145
Gewissheit (certainty), 54
God/s, 56, 78, 101;
  allows beings to be, 145;
  and ceremony, 25–26;
  and confession, 151;
  and creation, 40;
  and trust and faith, 130;
  as Creator, 60, 146;
  as disclosed, 15, 19;
  as near, 146;
  as social customs, 92;
  as sustainer, 16;
  before, 78, 128, 151–52;
  children of, 8;
  connection to, 43;
  determined by, 43;
  existence of, 153–54;
  Kingdom of, 124, 150–51;
  knowledge of, 146–47;
  obedient to, 145;
  relation to human beings, 53, 55–
    56, 63–65, 76–77;
  self as manifestation of, 16;
  underlying reason, 150;
  we are known by, 146;
  See also allowed to be/live;
    Divine Providence; Kingdom of
    God
God-centeredness, 64. *See also* ego-
  centered
great compassion, the, 144
great elements (earth, water, fire,
  wind), 65. *See Also* Buddhism:
  four great agents of
Greek, 9, 51–52, 54, 150
ground of being, 78–79

Hasa, Shōtō, viii, ix (note 2)
Hasidism, 93
heaven, 6, 8–9, 10, 14, 15–16, 17, 94,
  127;
  and earth, 8–9, 11, 13, 19, 128,
    130, 136, 143;

different from earth, 67;
hell and, 66;
path of, 129;
way of, 77
"Heaven Knows" ("...and the earth
  [also] knows"), 11, 92, 94–95, 126,
  127–28, 130, 136, 141, 146, 152
Heidegger, Martin, 1, 2, 6, 12, 15, 48
hippies, 122
historical consciousness, 41–45, 51,
  59, 61;
  arising from the Renaissance, 62;
  intrinsic to Christianity, 58;
  lack in Buddhism, 39–40, 63
Historie (history), distinguished from
  Geschichte, 74–75
history, and change, 8;
  and Christianity, 9, 41;
  and Indian thought, 50;
  and knowledge, 60;
  and nature, 105;
  and Protestantism, 40;
  and the Renaissance and Refor-
    mation, 4–8;
  and superhistory, 49;
  and understanding, 75;
  as Divine Providence, 60;
  as karma, 125;
  as reform or revolution, 42;
  as succession of nows, 50;
  basic form of, 134;
  beginnings of, 40;
  birth of historical consciousness,
    40–41;
  end of, 40;
  entering into, 61;
  in Buddhism, 106–7;
  lack of enthusiasm for in Buddhism,
    39, 52;
  meaning of, 74;
  of America, 120–22;
  past, present, future, 75–76;
  science of, 41–42, 60–61;
  unchangeableness and fashion-
    ableness, 73;
  where human life is carried on, 43

hōben (a temporary expedient, a
skill of means), 156
Holy Path, gate of the, 146
Hōnen, 56
Horen, Seiki, 6, 20 (note 3)
Hua-yen school, 52
human being/s, and the body, 81–86;
and the land, 124;
and privacy, 131–32;
and togetherness, 141;
as historical, 76, 134;
as problematic, 144–45;
authentic, 114–15;
characteristics of, 115–16;
connection to the environment, 98;
irreplaceability of, 92, 113;
karma at the root of. See karma;
relationships between, 76–77;
trustworthiness of, 77–79
human body, and human relations,
81–86;
and mind, 83–85;
and nature, 98, 103;
and religious land, 106;
and testimony, 121;
as four great agents, 65–66;
as a thou, 81–82, 103;
more than material, 81, 98, 103
human existence, and conscience, 94;
and nature, 98, 103;
and the Pure Land, 107;
and truth, 129;
and the unchangeable, 134–35;
as activity, 138;
as historical, 68, 71, 74, 76, 134;
as individual, 89–90;
as standing out of oneself, 138;
is historical, 68, 71, 74, 76;
problem of, 72;
world as field of, 100
human relation/s, 1, 116, 151;
and consciousness, 127;
and the family, 118, 124;
and the human body, 86;
and the ideal, 17;
and the self, 131, 145;

and social relations, 131–34;
and trustworthiness, 10–11, 77,
82–83, 140–41;
as central, 15;
as fourfold, 15–16, 136;
as I-thou, 82, 93;
as the unchangeable, 86–87, 134–
35;
authentic, 1, 80, 100, 114, 127, 130,
133. See also conscience;
like a secret room, 136;
types of, 83;
undermining of, 82
humanitas, 43

"I," 10, 55, 80–81, 91, 93, 102–3, 132;
as self-centered consciousness,
142, 145;
"this is 'I'," 146
"I am," 11, 80–82, 91, 100, 140, 145;
as irreplaceable individual, 11, 91;
See also human being: essential
feature
"I and thou" relationship, 10, 11, 12,
80, 81, 82, 83, 89, 92–93, 96–97,
99, 102, 103, 105–6
idealism, 120;
vs spiritualism, 68
ignorance, 148–49;
consciousness of, 15, 18, 148–49
I-it, relationship, 96–97, 98–99
ikikata (a way of living ones life),
25
Impure Land, 13, 14, 66–67, 106–7,
125. See also Pure Land, the
incarnation, of spirit, 121
individualism, Western, 1–2
individuality, 89–94, 104, 133. See
also "the single one";
relationship with universality, 89–
92
individual/particular/universal, 97
inochi (life), as ordered, 128–29
interconnectedness, 5

interdependent origination, 13, 100–1, 102, 106;
  cause-effect relation, 101–2;
  vs physics, 106
I-thou. *See* "I and thou"
izukalae (whereto), 24

Japanese Religiosity, Van Bragt's, 20 (note 2)
Jesus, 24, 29, 67;
  and conscience, 150–51
ji (the viewpoint of actuality), 91–92
jinen (formless true reality), 13, 106, 107
jiriki (self-power), 43. *See* self-power
jitafuni (self and others are not two), 139
jōdo (the Pure Land), 8
Judaism, 150
"*Juryōbon*," Dōgen's ("Buddha's Span of Life"), 155

Kamakura period (1185–1333), 9, 32, 45 (note 2), 47
Kamo River, 65
Kant, Immanuel, 12
karma (universal law of act and consequence), 14, 78, 123, 135–36;
  at the root of a human being, 125–26;
  and ethics, 126;
  "threefold karma of body, speech, and mind," 135–36
kata (form), 4, 24–26, 28
Keene, Donald, 20 (note 8)
Kierkegaard, Søren, and subjectivity, 11, 89, 91–93, 134
kihō (believing mind), 87
Kingdom of God (also Kingdom of Heaven), 8, 9–10, 14, 66, 67, 84, 86, 122, 123, 124, 125, 150–51.
  See also Pure Land, the
kite analogy, 4–5, 35, 36
knowledge, and Christianity, 64;
  acquired by one's self, 57–58, 62–64, 68, 193–94, 136, 143, 148;

and conscience, 15–16, 56, 93, 145;
and logic, 90–91;
and truth or truthfulness, 129;
and universals, 90–91;
as historical, 42, 61;
as self-consciousness, 137–38, 140, 146;
authentic, 46, 148;
by means of the body, 56–58, 81, 104–5;
direct, 9;
good, 112;
intimate knowledge of, 141–42;
"know thyself." *See* "know thyself";
knowing things as they are, 99;
of dharma, 147;
of not-knowing, 18–19;
of our subjectivity, 102;
of true facts, 60–61, 63–64;
of the world, 63, 65, 68;
scholar's, 105;
scientific, 44, 54, 56–57, 61–62, 98, 102, 104–5, 129;
See also self-knowledge
"know thyself," Socrates' dictum, 12, 19, 95, 148–49
kōshikondō (to mix up public and private matters), 132
koto (a work), 139
Kraemer, Professor H., 52–53
kyōgaibetsuden (the use of self-power [*jiriki*] in Zen Buddhism to achieve enlightenment), 56
Kyōgyōshinshō, Shinran's, 23, 26
Kyoto school, 1

land, 85;
  and the great elements, 65;
  and the human body, 84, 103–4;
  and sentient beings, 123;
  as place where human beings are related, 86, 123–24;
  as place where we are allowed to live, 125. *See also* allowed to be/live;

as symbol, 123;
connected to Buddha-nature, 87–88;
corrupt vs. Pure land, 66, 68, 124–25;
different from earth, 67;
land of God, 123;
"Land of the Buddhas," 66, 84, 86, 88, 123;
love of, 14. *See also* love;
Nishitani's discussion of, 13–14;
of the country, 104, 106, 123;
See also *Blut und Boden*; Pure Land
Last Judgment, 41
Last Writings: Nothingness and the Religious Worldview, Nishida's, 20 (note 5)
liberalism, 39
logic, 90–92
logos, 90–91, 149
Lotus Sūtra, 66, 155
love, a stone or a tree, 12, 97. *See also* I and thou;
in marriage, 116–17;
of Buddhism, viii;
of the land, 14;
of nature, 13
Luther, Martin, 11, 54, 56, 62;
and conscience, 53

machines, 98, 100, 104–5
Mahāyāna. *See* Buddhism
makoto (truthfulness), 129
mānovijñānā (realization), 142
marriage, 78–79, 116–17, 118
Marxism, 42, 153, 154–55
materialism, Western, 1;
atheistic, 1–2
meaning, authentic, 27, 29, 78;
of *kata*, 28
medical science and technique, 98–99
Meiji era (1868–1912), 31, 35, 51, 111
Middle Ages, 43, 44, 52, 53, 151, 154;
historical way of thinking branded as heretical, 41

Middle Path, Buddhist. *See under* Buddhism
mind, 17;
and body, 57, 82–86;
and Christianity, 150–51;
and conscience, 111–12, 130;
and disclosure, 83, 142–43;
and doubt, 54;
and ethics, 83;
and *logos*, 149;
and no-mindedness, 18–19;
and place, 84;
and trust, 140–41;
as Buddha-nature, 16–17, 113–14;
as empty, 15, 144, 147;
as good, 111–12, 137;
as open, 79;
authentic, 142;
culture of, 175;
ground of, 113;
new, 150–51;
settles down (*anshinritsumei*), 129;
springs from nature, 101;
See also Buddhism
Miroku, the bodhisattva, 13, 106–7
miso soup, 103–4
modernism (postmodernism), 1, 3–5
modernity, three forces shaping, 44, 52
modernization, and tradition, 34–36, 63–64, 71;
and Buddhism, 2, 36–38, 63–64, 69–73, 88;
and human existence, 72;
difficulties posed by, 2;
influence of Western culture, 37;
See also westernization
modern world, 62;
and alienation, 10;
and Buddhism, 9, 40;
and Christianity, 39, 63–64;
and historical consciousness, 61;
and subjective self-awareness, 59;
and technology, 35, 62–63;
and tradition, 29–30;
characteristics of, 42, 44, 52;

modern world *(continued)*
  religion and, 2, 5;
  See also knowledge: acquired by
    one's self
monpō (to listen to Buddha's
  teaching), 71–72
Mount Hiei, monks climbing down
  from, 9, 32, 45 (note 2), 47

Namu Amida Butsu ("I Take Refuge
  in Amida Buddha"), 6, 7. See
  also *nembutsu*
natural sciences, 43, 44–45, 52, 61–
  63, 97–98, 99, 100;
  and experimentation, 44;
  function and substance, 99–100
nature, 8, 16, 20 (note 8), 146;
  and experimentation, 44;
  and technology, 12, 61–63;
  as constructed, 102–3;
  as divinely created, 43;
  as a field, 100;
  as material-at-hand, 12–13;
  as organic whole, 101;
  come back to, 105–6;
  humans as part of, 13, 16, 98–100;
  intrinsic value of, 5–6;
  love of, 13. *See also* love;
  struggle against, 13, 61–62, 105
Nazis (National Socialist Party), and
  patriotism, 14, 123
nembutsu (prayers to Buddha), 25.
  See also Namu Amida Butsu
Neo-Confucian school, 16
Newton, Sir Isaac, 104
Nichiren sect of Buddhism, 45 (note 2)
Nietzsche, F., 3, 67
nihilism, vii, 3, 5, 154–55, 156;
  as the root of modernism, 3, 5
nihilum. See Buddhism: *nihilum*
ningen (human being, person), 16
nirvāna (reality), 10, 13, 17, 107,
  155–56. *See also* samsāra
Nirvāna Sūtra, 87
Nishida, Kitarō (1870–1945), vii, 1,
  7, 10–11, 15, 20 (note 5)

"Nishitani on Japanese Religiosity,"
  Van Bragt's, 20 (note 2)
no-mind, no-mindedness, 7, 11, 18,
  19 , 144. *See also* self-negation
nonclergy and nonlaity, 32–33, 34, 47
nondualism, Buddhist, 10, 18, 79–80,
  93
nonself. *See* no-self
nori (a law), 91
no-self/nonself, 11, 18, 19, 79–80,
  87–88, 93. *See also* egoless;
  no-selfhood-like subjectivity, 79–80;
  absence of, 97
nothingness, 13, 48, 80, 102, 143–44.
  See also Buddhism: and emptiness; Buddhism: *nihilum*;
  emptiness

Obaku Zen Buddhism, 7
ontology, 80
open-mindedness, and trust, 79
other-centeredness, instead of ego-
  centeredness, 79. *See also* ego-
  centeredness
other-power (*tariki*), 6–8, 88, 144;
  vs self-power, 6, 7. *See also* self-
  power
ōyake (the public), 132

parable, of the famous good
  physician, 155–56
path, to go along a, 144–45;
  ethics as the ought-to-be path; 118;
  See also Buddhism: and the
    middle path; Sacred Path
Pharisees, 150
physics, 81, 106
Plato, 89, 148, 150
politics, 125;
  and human rights, 39;
  and Puritanism, 119;
  in America, 122;
  power politics, 133
pollution, environmental, 61, 98–99

power, 121, 144, 152–53;
Buddha's, 87;
family, 117;
negation of (hollowed), 143–44;
of Buddha's Law, 121;
of Buddhism, viii, 32;
of human freedom, 60;
of Japan, 35;
of nature, 13, 61, 124;
of religion, 39, 122–23;
of science and technology, 2, 44;
of social ethics, 39, 119;
of tradition, 4–6, 29, 36;
of virtue, 143;
of the West, 37;
other-power (*tariki*). *See* other-power;
political, 133;
saving, 143–44;
self-power (*jiriki*). *See* self-power;
universal, 7;
See also *Gewalt*
practice, 45 (note 2);
and interpersonal relationships, 1;
and the invocation of Amida Buddha, 87;
and self-realization, 61;
and trustworthiness, 77;
as constant renovation, 42;
as a spiritual void, 121–122;
disciplinary, 53;
faith-practice-testimony, 59;
religious, 26, 144;
unified practice, 7, 42
Protestantism, 8, 39, 41, 128;
and capitalism, 39
psychology, 16, 113
Pure Land, the, viii, ix (note 2), 6–7, 9–10, 13–14, 17, 66–68, 86, 88, 106–7, 123, 125, 146, 155;
different from the earth, 67;
gate, 130;
sect of Buddhism, ix, 6–7, 11, 20 (note 1), 87, 99, 137, 143. *See also* Shin Buddhism;
See also Kingdom of God; other-power; Shinran

Puritanism, 119–22, 129–30;
impotent tradition, 121–22

realization. *See* self-realization
reason, 19, 91, 114, 149–50
reconstruct, to come back to origins, 4, 28–29
reevaluate, religious services and doctrines, 27. *See also* Buddhism: attempt to reappropriate
Reformation, the, 8–9, 41, 43, 53, 55, 62;
as the foundation of capitalism and liberalism, 39;
and faith, 55
reidanjichi (direct experience), 56–57, 136
relationship/s, genuine (human), 1, 10, 15, 134
Religion and Nothingness, Nishitani's, vi, viii, 1
religious knowledge, different from discursive thinking, 56–58
religious organizations, 29, 154;
and the family, 24;
and founding teachings of, 3;
and the general public, 65;
and historical understanding, 52;
become ego-centered, 8–9, 47–48, 64;
becoming indifferent to, 32;
modernization of, 36;
stepping inside of, 5–6, 23, 45;
stepping outside of, 4, 8–9, 23, 32, 47
Renaissance, 8, 43–44, 62–63;
and the rise of historical consciousness, 43
repentance, 150–51
res (the cause, the real) *See koto*
resignation, 59–60. *See also* fatalism
revolution, as constant renovation, 3–4, 42–43
ri (reason), 17, 91, 114
"rice cakes painted on paper." *See* sūtras

rihō (the rational law), 90–91
rin (fellows), 17, 114
rinri (ethics), 17, 114
ritual, 3, 9, 121
Roman, 9, 51
ryōchi (good knowledge), 112
ryōnō (good intellect), 112
ryōshin (good mind, conscience), 16, 111–13, 137. *See also* Buddha-nature; conscience; ethics
ryūkō (fashionable), 135

Sabbath, 150
Sacred Path, the, 130
sacred-secular, the two-truths doctrine, 73, 107
salvation, the doctrine of, 17, 18, 113
samsāra (the empirical world), 10, 17. *See also* nirvāna
Sangha (the community of Buddhist monks), 47, 48–50, 52
San-lun school, 52, 80
science/s, 1–3;
    and the body, 103–6;
    and faith, 57–58;
    and history, 41–43, 60–61;
    and Japan, 4–5;
    and materialism, 65, 67;
    the natural. *See* natural sciences;
    and power, 143;
    the social. *See* social sciences;
    and subjectivity, 12, 44;
    concerned with knowledge, 54, 62, 137;
    rise of, 1;
    substance and function in, 95–100
sect, religious, 25–26
secularism, 4
secularized, ethics, 8;
    view of the world, 8;
    world, 5
self, 19, 139, 146–47;
    Buddhist, 18;
    nonegoic, 18

self-awareness, 58–59, 65, 68, 134, 139–40, 141–42, 143–45, 146, 147, 152;
    and the dictum "to be alone," 142;
    in Buddhism, 146;
    historical, connected with knowledge of the world, 65;
    of personality, 59
self-centered/ness, viii, 97, 138–39, 142, 145. *See also* ego-centered
self-knowledge, 19, 55, 137–38, 146–47, 152. *See also* consciousness: self-; self-realization
self-negation, 7. *See also* no-mindedness
self-power (*jiriki*), 6–8, 43–44, 88, 144. *See also* other-power
self-realization, 9, 17, 18, 20 (note 8), 43, 58, 87. *See also* enlightenment; self-knowledge;
    of the individual, 55
self-reliance, and trust, 79–80
shin (mind), 112
Shin Buddhism, 6, 9–10, 14, 20 (note 1), 24, 25, 33, 50, 59, 105, 106, 155. *See also* Pure Land
Shin Buddhism: Japan's Major Religious Contribution to the West, D. T. Suzuki's, 7, 20 (note 3, 4)
Shingon, sect of Buddhism, 25, 65
Shinran (1173–1262), 6, 23–24, 29, 45 (note 2), 56, 88, 107, 137
Shintoism, 9, 23, 51
shiriau (to be acquainted with each other), 141–42
Shōbōgenzō, Dōgen's, 23–24, 48. *See also* Dōgen
shōjōjū (assured of becoming a Buddha), 106
shōzōmatsu (tripartite scheme of Buddhist theory), 40–41
sin, 41, 151–52
"skill of means." *See under* Buddhism
Smith, Adam, 39

social ethics, 43–45;
    and Buddhism, 38–39, 51–52, 59, 63;
    and Christianity, 119;
    and Confucianism, 15;
    and enlightenment, 17;
    and faith, 56;
    and syncretism, 51;
    and trust, 78–79;
    West's demand for, 8
social relations, 126, 131–32, 133–34
social sciences, 85–86, 99, 143, 154–55;
    and functionality, 99–100;
    of history, 60, 61
society/ies, 6, 62–63, 85, 147;
    a higher "public," 128;
    and change, 31, 130;
    and conscience, 95, 127;
    and human relationships, 100,
        116, 126, 131;
    and modern problems, 2, 117;
    and nature, 103;
    and Socrates, 15;
    British, 119;
    continual rebuilding of, 60;
    gap in, 5;
    Japanese, 35;
    Kierkegaard's critique of, 92;
    Puritan, 120;
    revolution in, 42;
    search for new, 59;
    something common in, 132–33
sociology, 85
Socrates, 12, 15, 18, 19, 95, 148–51,
    153, 154;
    "Know thyself," 12, 19, 95, 148–49
Soga, Ryogin, 20 (note 1)
sola fide (by faith alone), 56
Sophists, 148
Sources of Japanese Tradition,
    Tsnunoda, De Bary and
    Keene's, 20 (note 8)
Spae, Joseph, J., 20 (note 2)
spiritualism, vs idealism, 68
struggle, with nature. See under
    nature

student, movement, 45 (note 1),
    129–30;
    revolt, ix, 28, 143, 148, 154
subjectivity, ix, 11–13, 18, 44, 79–80,
    85, 87–89, 91–93, 95, 102–3, 134,
    141, 153
subject/object, 10–11, 20 (note 8),
    44, 80–81, 89, 90–93, 96–97, 138–
    39, 140, 147. See also "I and
    thou"
suchness. See Buddhism: and
    suchness
sumanai (things are left unfinished),
    128
suneidesis (conscience/knowledge), 54
Sung period (960–1279), 111–12
suprahistorical, 72
sūtras (Buddhist scriptures), 25, 56,
    107, 133, 154;
    as "rice cakes painted on paper,"
        9, 56
Suzuki, D. T., 6, 7, 20 (note 3), 53

Tang period (618–907), 111–12
Tannishō, Shinran's, 23, 24, 29
tariki. See other-power
Tathāgata (thus come, thus gone),
    87–88, 106.
tathatā (suchness), 143. See also
    Buddhism: and suchness
technology, 1, 2–3, 4–5, 12, 35, 61–
    62, 63, 105
testimony, 58–59, 107, 121, 130, 135,
    137, 144–45;
    involved in faith, 58–59;
    tied up with "to go along a
        path," 144–45
theology, 53–54, 55, 73–74
"The Problem of Japanese Culture,"
    Nishida's, 20
"the single one," Kierkegaard's, 89,
    91
Thou, the Absolute, 11
Threefold Relationship, the, 133–34
Tiantai school, 52, 80

togetherness, 83, 93, 141
Tokugawa era (1615–1868), 24, 31,
    51
tomodachi (friend), 141
tradition, 119, 121;
    and the future, 75–76, 107;
    and modernization, 5, 34–36, 71;
    as old-fashioned, 68;
    as reconstruction, 29–30, 34;
    destruction of, 27–28, 29;
    Greek, 150;
    Jewish, 93;
    power of, 35;
    return to, 2–6;
    revitalization of, 34–35, 28–29, 92;
    skin of, 31
true self, 16
trust, 10–11, 15, 18–19, 55–56, 79–80,
    82, 88, 130, 140–41;
    mutual, 77, 85, 87, 95
trustworthiness, ix, 10, 15, 18, 76,
    77–80;
    and human relations, 82–83;
    mutual, 86–87;
    something unchangeable, 87
truth, 3, 7, 9–10, 16, 20 (note 8), 26–
    27, 30, 66, 68, 71, 99, 104, 119–
    20, 122, 129, 135, 143, 149;
    religious, eternal and unchange-
    able, 72–73
truthfulness, 10, 11, 77, 79, 86–87,
    129–30, 152. *See also* conscience;
    makoto;
    authentic, 134
tsukemono (a kind of pickle), 103
Tsunoda, Ryusaku, 20 (note 8)

uncertainty, 54–55
unchangeable, 10, 41, 58, 72–73, 86–
    87, 134–35;
    and fashionable. See *fuekiryūkō*;
    history: unchangeableness and
    fashionableness
universality, 89–91, 104. *See also*
    individuality

Wang, Yang-ming, 16;
    and Buddhist aloofness, 112–13;
    and conscience, 16, 56, 131;
    Buddhist influence on, 112;
    as critical of Buddhism, 112;
    his *Denshūroku*, 112
watakushi (privacy), 132
water and waves, 102
Watsuji, Tetsurō, 10, 16, 103
way of life/living, 9, 24–25, 29, 32,
    43, 53. *See also kata*;
    and the body, 57;
    and divestment, 31;
    and modernization, 34, 36;
    and mundane affairs, 112;
    and religion, 33–34;
    an essential characteristic of, 42;
    as historical, 40;
    basic, 116;
    concern of religion, 27, 29–30, 44;
    genuine, 30;
    knowledge realized in, 57;
    map of, 4;
    new, 37;
    reinterpretation of, 34;
    revitalization of, 3, 28–29, 60
Weber, Max, 128
westernization, difficulties posed by, 2;
    of Japan, 35. *See also* moderniza-
    tion
wissen (to know), 54, 145

Yin-yuan, Lung-chi, 7
Yōmeigaku, school of, 112
yū (unity of knowledge and deed), 138

Zen Buddhism 25;
    and Buddha-mind, 113;
    and Confucianism, 112;
    and direct transmission, 56;
    and discipline, 132;
    and enlightenment, 57, 133;
    and foolishness, 105;
    and the ground of mind, 113;
    and the land, 66;

and nomindedness, 11;
and Obaku Zen, 7;
and self-power, 158;
and Wang-yang Ming, 56, 112;

as direct experience, 17, 57;
as salvation through works, 113;
the individual as private, 132
Zuimonki, Dōgen's, 23